THE KING & ME

Dr. Derrick Love

Becoming More Like Jesus One Day at a Time

DR. DERRICK LOVE

THE KING & ME

Dr. Derrick Love

ISBN (Paperback): 979-8-9989822-0-0
ISBN (Hardcover): 979-8-9989822-1-7

For permissions, inquiries, or bulk orders, contact the publisher:

NEW HORIZON
EDUCATIONAL INSTITUTE, LLC

New Horizon Educational Institute, LLC

All scripture quotations, unless otherwise indicated, are taken from the Holy Bible, New International Version®.

Layout and design by New Horizon Educational Institute, LLC. Printed in the United States of America

Special Bonus Resource:
Upon purchasing this book, you are entitled to access a free downloadable resource: The King & Me 60-Day Affirmation Cards, available in both print-able and digital formats.

To claim your free resource, please visit: https://newhorizoninstitute.org/

Dedication

To my wife, your love has been a steady anchor in every storm and a living reflection of grace I know I did not deserve, sustaining me in seasons of pressure and reminding me that covenant is strengthened not in ease but in endurance. To my children, I pray that your lives continually reflect the God who sees you fully, shapes you patiently, and sends you boldly into purpose, and I ask that these words plant something eternal in your hearts that will guide you long after my voice grows quiet. To my parents, thank you for building your faith into mine through countless quiet sacrifices, consistent prayers, and unseen acts of obedience that laid a foundation stronger than I understood at the time. And to the friends, mentors, and companions who have walked with me in the trenches, your encouragement, your honest correction, and your faithful presence have carried more weight than you will ever truly know.

This work is born from your steadfast support, your shared journeys, and the resilience you modeled through both triumph and trial. It stands as a testimony that none of us are formed in isolation and that God uses community, hardship, and hope together as instruments of refinement. My prayer is that it serves as a reminder that God is not finished forming us, that His process is intentional, and that He never wastes the very experiences that shape us into who we are becoming.

"Being confident of this, that He who began a good work in you will carry it on to completion until the day of Christ Jesus," Philippians 1:6.

To the reader, understand that you do not need perfection to begin this journey, nor do you need complete clarity before taking the next faithful step. What you need is the courage to remain when it would be easier to retreat and the humility to allow God to shape you through every season. This journey is now yours to walk, so move deliberately, stay present to the process, and allow it to change you in ways only God can design.

TABLE OF
CONTENTS

Introduction

What if the most important transformation of your life wasn't loud, public, or instant? What if it were quiet, gradual, and completely sacred?

We live in a culture obsessed with outcomes: fast results, polished images, and highlight reels. But the Kingdom of God grows in different ways. It grows in secret. It forms in stillness. It shapes us through surrender, not striving.

There is a hunger in every human soul, a deep, unshakable longing to live for something more. Not more busyness or success or applause. But more of what actually matters. More peace. More clarity. More connection. More of God.

If you're holding this devotional, it's likely because you feel that stirring. Maybe you've walked with Jesus for years and sense that He's inviting you deeper. Or maybe your faith has felt routine or fragile lately, and you're craving a reset. You're not alone. And you're not here by accident.

The Christian life isn't about arriving at a perfect version of yourself. It's about becoming more like Jesus. Not just knowing about Him but being shaped by Him, formed into His likeness from the inside out. It's about trading shallow religion for real relationship, daily surrender, and spiritual transformation. That's what *The King & Me* is all about.

This is a 60-day invitation to meet with God, hear His voice, and allow His Spirit to reshape your character, your thinking, and your habits. Each day will guide you through Scripture, reflection, prayer, and a practical application designed to help you live more fully and freely in the presence of the King.

But this isn't about checking boxes or adding another spiritual task to your already busy life. It's not about perfection or pressure, it's about presence. It's about choosing to pause long enough to remember who God is, who you are in Him, and what really matters.

Jesus came to establish a Kingdom and to invite you into it. But the Kingdom isn't built through performance; it's built through intimacy. It's formed in quiet moments of trust, honesty, repentance, and worship. In the everyday decisions to obey, to love, to forgive, to grow.

You were never meant to drift through life or live on spiritual auto-pilot. You were created to reflect the heart of the King. Over the next sixty days, you'll be invited to deepen your roots, examine your heart, confront distractions, and walk in new freedom. You'll explore what it means to be humble, courageous, surrendered, generous, and spiritually grounded. You'll wrestle with truth, rest in grace, and rise in purpose.

There will be days when the reflection comforts you. Days when it challenges you. And days when it stretches something inside you that needed to grow. Don't rush the process. Some days will feel like a breakthrough. Others may feel quiet or even uncomfortable. But every day is an opportunity to become more fully alive in Christ.

Come with your whole heart, your faith, your doubts, your dreams, your weariness. God doesn't need a polished version of you. He wants the real you. Because real transformation only happens when we show up honestly and let the King meet us in our becoming.

You are not just a servant in His Kingdom. You are a child of the King. And He is ready to walk with you.

So let this be your prayer at the start of every day: **"Jesus, shape me. Lead me. Make me more like You."**

The journey begins now. Let's walk it together.

How to Use This Devotional

This devotional is designed to walk with you, one day at a time, into deeper transformation.

Each day includes:

- **A Scripture** to anchor your heart.
- **A reflection** to encourage, challenge, or reframe your perspective.
- **An application or prayer** to help you put truth into motion.
- **Reflection questions** to help you engage more personally.

Here are a few suggestions to get the most out of this journey:

1. **Set aside 10–15 minutes a day.** Consistency is more powerful than intensity. Whether it's morning, midday, or night, find a rhythm that works for you.

2. **Journal your responses.** Keep a notebook or digital journal nearby to write down thoughts, prayers, or anything God reveals.

3. **Be honest.** Don't rush past the hard questions. God isn't looking for the right answers; He's looking for a real heart.

4. **Pray through each entry.** Let the words become dialogue. Invite the Holy Spirit to speak specifically to you.

5. **Share with a friend or group.** Spiritual growth multiplies in community. Consider walking through this with a friend or small group for deeper accountability and encouragement.

6. **Take your time.** This is not a race. Feel free to linger on a day if it speaks deeply to your soul.

Whether you move through this in 50 days or over the course of a few months, the goal remains the same: to let the King shape who you are becoming.

WEEK 1

DAY 1
Mirrors Are Brutal Things

Scripture

"And we all, who with unveiled faces contemplate the Lord's glory, are being transformed into his image with ever-increasing glory..."

2 Corinthians 3:18 (NIV)

Reflection

Mirrors do not lie, but they rarely flatter, and if we are honest, most of us avoid the one that matters most. We love the idea of being made in God's image because it sounds noble and sacred, as though we are naturally glowing with spiritual potential. However, that is not how a mirror functions because it does not project what could be; it reflects what is.

Much of what appears in that reflection is not glorious. It can be petty, defensive, anxious, addicted to attention, and allergic to silence. It forgives only when convenient, loves selectively, and obeys God in theory while negotiating in practice.

Here is the difficult truth: you are being shaped by something at all times. If not Christ, then culture. If not the Spirit, then your habits, your ego, your trauma, or your timeline. Transformation is not optional because it is simply a matter of who is doing the shaping.

When Paul writes that we are being transformed into His image, he is not describing cosmetic improvement but a process that requires the removal of what does not belong. Sanctification is not a filter but a renovation of the soul. Unlike social media, God is not interested in curating your best angles.

Jesus' image is not serene. It is the image of a man who refused revenge, who held His tongue while being falsely accused, and who chose obedience over comfort. If that is the image into which we are being shaped, we should not expect comfort. You are not being invited to admire Jesus; you are being asked to resemble Him. Resemblance means suffering as He suffered, forgiving as He forgave, speaking truth as He spoke truth, and loving those who do not deserve it.

There will be days when this process feels more like erasure than growth and when everything you thought defined you is being stripped away. Those moments are not failures but chisels shaping something truer beneath the surface. If you allow the Spirit to continue carving, what will emerge will not be a better version of you but a reflection of someone else entirely.

Like the one who stood before the mirror and whispered that the image had been distorted yet desired it back, healing begins not with clarity but with confession.

Application

Stand in front of a mirror and do not adjust your face or fix your posture. Simply look and acknowledge aloud that this is the image you have been given, that you have distorted it, and that you want it restored. Then write down one aspect of your heart, behavior, or inner life that least resembles Christ, and be specific. Instead of saying you could be more loving, identify where you withhold affection as a form of punishment. That is where the Spirit begins His work.

Prayer

God, I've confused affirmation with transformation. I've spent years tweaking my image while ignoring Yours. But I don't want a flattering reflection. I want a faithful one. Cut away what doesn't belong to You. Even if it leaves scars. Make me a mirror that tells the truth, not about me, but about You. Amen.

Guide Your Thinking:

1. *What is shaping me more right now, culture, fear, habit, or Christ?*

2. *Where in my life do I most resist looking like Jesus?*

3. *Am I willing to be reshaped, even if it costs me the image, I've carefully curated?*

_____

_____

_____

_____

_____

_____

_____

_____

_____

_____

_____

_____

_____

_____

_____

_____

DAY 2
The Heart of Humility

Scripture

"In your relationships with one another, have the same mindset as Christ Jesus."

Philippians 2:5 (NIV)

Reflection

If you want to know what the Kingdom of God looks like, start with humility. It's not loud. It doesn't demand attention. It's not performative or insecure. It's a quiet strength that flows from knowing who you are and, more importantly, *whose* you are.

In a culture obsessed with recognition and achievement, humility can feel unnatural, even risky. But in the Kingdom of God, it's the foundation of trans-formation. It's the soil where obedience grows, where grace flows, and where pride dies so that love can live.

Jesus is our model. Though He was fully God, He chose the path of humility. He laid down His rights, His status, and His glory to serve those who could offer Him nothing in return. He didn't just *speak* with authority; He *stooped* in compassion. He washed feet. He welcomed children. He touched the unclean. And ultimately, He humbled Himself all the way to the cross.

Humility isn't self-hatred or false modesty. It's not pretending you're less than you are. It's simply seeing yourself clearly through the eyes of God, fully loved, completely dependent on grace, and deeply aware that every gift, strength, or influence you carry is from Him, for Him, and about Him.

John the Baptist expressed it perfectly: *"He must become greater; I must become less."* (John 3:30). That's the heart of humility, not a loss of identity, but a willing surrender of self-importance. A life that points to Jesus, not ourselves.

Humility also shows up in our relationships. It's in how we listen, how we speak, how we handle offense, and how quickly we forgive. It's being more eager to understand than to win. It's admitting when we're wrong, choosing grace over gossip, and serving when no one notices.

If we want to grow spiritually, humility is non-negotiable. Without it, we resist correction, avoid dependence, and remain stagnant. But with it, our hearts stay soft, our ears stay open, and our lives become vessels God can use.

Application

Ask the Holy Spirit to gently reveal any prideful attitudes in your heart. Is there a place where you've been resistant to correction, quick to compare, or hesitant to serve?

Write down one practical way you can practice humility today, whether it's choosing silence in a moment of conflict, apologizing first, or serving without recognition.

Begin to pray daily: *"Jesus, teach me to become less, so that You may become more in me."*

Prayer

Lord, I want to reflect Your heart. Strip away my pride, my need to impress, and my fear of being unseen. Teach me to love humility as You do. Let me serve others with joy and walk in the quiet confidence that comes from knowing who I am in You. Make me more like You today. Amen.

Guide Your Thinking:

1. *Where is God calling me to practice humility today?*

2. *How does humility free me to serve others?*

_____

_____

_____

_____

_____

_____

_____

_____

_____

_____

_____

_____

_____

_____

_____

_____

DAY 3
Formed in the Fire, Growth in Trials

Scripture

"These trials will show that your faith is genuine. It is being tested as fire tests and purifies gold..."

1 Peter 1:7 (NLT)

Reflection

No one asks for trials. No one signs up for pain. But if you've walked with God for any length of time, you've likely discovered this truth: the fire that threatens to consume you is often the same fire God uses to *refine* you.

Trials test our faith not to break it, but to prove it. To purify it. To burn away what's false, shallow, or performative and reveal what is deep, real, and enduring. Like gold, faith is refined in heat. It glows brighter. It becomes more valuable. But it takes time. And it takes trust.

We often ask God to remove the fire. But what if the fire is what's forming us?

Think of Joseph, betrayed by family and forgotten in prison. Or when David was anointed as king but hunted in caves. Or Ruth, walking through grief and scarcity. Their trials didn't disqualify them; they *defined* them. Not because the fire was easy, but because they didn't walk through it alone.

God doesn't waste pain. Every season of waiting, every disappointment, every moment you've cried out and heard silence; He sees it all. And He is using it to shape something stronger in you. Trials often strip away what you thought you needed to reveal what your soul *actually* needs: Him.

Sometimes, growth looks like survival. Sometimes, it's waking up and still believing, still hoping, still showing up in prayer, even when everything in you wants to quit. That kind of faith, the kind that endures the furnace, is precious to God. And it's powerful.

Maybe your current fire is lost. Maybe it's uncertainty. Maybe it's internal battles no one sees. Wherever you are, know this: God is in the fire with you. He's not absent. He's refining. He's not punishing you. He's preparing you. And what feels like a setback may actually be setting the stage for deeper faith and greater glory.

You're not being destroyed. You're being formed.

Application

Reflect on a trial you're currently facing, or one you've recently come through. What has it exposed? What has it revealed about God, about yourself, about where your hope truly lies?

Write a prayer of honesty. Pour out your pain, but also invite God to use it for His purpose. Ask Him not just to deliver you from the fire, but to do something *in you* through it.

Prayer

God, I don't love the fire, but I trust You in it. I trust that You're doing more than I can see. That even in pain, You are present. Purify my faith. Remove what's shallow and shaky. Make me strong, not because life is easy, but because I am rooted in You. Use every trial to shape me into who You created me to be. Amen.

Guide Your Thinking:

1. *What has the fire of this season revealed in me that God wants to refine?*

2. *How can I lean into God in the trial rather than just praying to escape it?*

_____

_____

_____

_____

_____

_____

_____

_____

_____

_____

_____

_____

_____

_____

_____

DAY 4
Walking in Love

Scripture

"And walk in the way of love, just as Christ loved us and gave himself up for us."

Ephesians 5:2 (NIV)

Reflection

In a story shared in The Christian Post, a barefoot boy stood outside a shoe store in the cold, peering through the window. When a kind woman approached and learned he was praying for shoes, she brought him inside, gently washed his feet, and bought him a new pair. Overwhelmed by her kindness, he asked, "Ma'am, are you God's wife?" He had witnessed divine love embodied in her actions, love that gave without expecting anything in return.

This is the kind of love that Scripture calls us to. "Walk in the way of love," Paul writes, "just as Christ loved us and gave himself up for us." (Ephesians 5:2). This isn't a passive feeling or fleeting sentiment; it's an intentional, daily lifestyle modeled after Christ's sacrificial love.

There are two powerful expressions of Christ-like love in the Bible: agape, selfless, unconditional love, and philia, deep, relational love marked by loyalty and compassion. Jesus modeled both. He gave Himself completely on the cross (agape), and He shared intimate, caring friendship with His disciples (philia).

To walk in love means to embody both. It means showing kindness even when we are tired, choosing forgiveness over resentment, extending compassion when it's inconvenient, and building relationships that reflect God's grace. Love isn't measured by grand gestures but by everyday faithfulness, listening to someone when you're busy, choosing gentleness in an argument, or serving quietly when no one sees it.

This kind of love is rare in a world that often encourages self-interest, conditional relationships, and emotional distance. But when we love the way Christ loved, we become vessels of healing, reconciliation, and peace. Our love becomes a testimony, not of our own goodness but of God's love flowing through us.

What would change in your life if every decision were filtered through love? What relationships would be restored, what wounds healed, what burdens lifted? Walking in love means reflecting the heart of Christ so clearly that others, like that little boy, begin to wonder if we might be related to God, because His love is unmistakable in us.

Application

Ask God to reveal someone who needs His love through you today. Choose one way to express love, whether through an encouraging word, an act of service, or a thoughtful gesture. Reflect in your journal on how walking in love changes your perspective and strengthens relationships.

Prayer

Lord, I confess it's easier to love in theory than in practice. But You've called me to walk, not just think or feel, but walk in love. Help me to move toward others with patience, grace, and generosity. Teach me to forgive quickly, speak kindly, and serve joyfully. Let my life reflect Your heart so vividly that others see You through me. Fill my spirit with the courage to love as You love, sacrificially, endlessly, and without reservation. Amen.

Guide Your Thinking:

1. *Who needs to experience God's love through me today?*

2. *How can I grow in both agape and philia love?*

_____

_____

_____

_____

_____

_____

_____

_____

_____

_____

_____

_____

_____

_____

_____

DAY 5
Choosing Stillness in a Noisy World

Scripture

"Be still, and know that I am God..."

Psalm 46:10 (NIV)

Reflection

We live in a world that doesn't know how to be still. From the moment we wake up, we are bombarded by sound notifications, news, noise, and endless demands. Silence is rare. Stillness feels unproductive. And yet, it is often in stillness that we hear the voice of God most clearly.

Stillness is not just the absence of movement. It's a posture of the heart. It's choosing to quiet the chaos, not just around you, but within you. It's pausing long enough to remember that God is God... and you are not.

In Scripture, the command to "be still" isn't just a gentle suggestion; it's a call to surrender. To stop striving. To let go of the need to fix, to perform, or to figure it all out. It's an invitation to step out of anxiety and into awe. To remember that God is already at work before you rush, before you speak, before you do anything else.

Jesus modeled this beautifully. Despite the demands of His ministry, He regularly withdrew to quiet places. Not because He was avoiding responsibility, but because He knew the power of solitude. He knew that stillness with the Father was the source of strength for everything else.

But we resist stillness, don't we? We stay busy to feel important. We fill every moment, so we don't have to face what's beneath the surface. But stillness has a way of revealing what distraction hides: our fears, our wounds, our deepest needs.

And yet, this is where God meets us, not in our hustle, but in our hush. In the quiet space where we stop talking to Him and start listening to Him.

Stillness doesn't mean we abandon our responsibilities. It means we anchor our souls before we face them. It's choosing presence over panic, rest over rush, and awareness over anxiety. It's making room for God, not just in crisis, but in the cadence of every day.

Application

Set aside 10 to 15 minutes today to sit in complete stillness, free from music, notifications, and the pull of multitasking, and simply be present in quiet. Begin by focusing intentionally on your breathing, slowing your inhale and exhale, and then gently pray, "Be still and know that You are God," allowing those words to move from your mind into your heart.

Resist the urge to rush through the moment or treat it as another task to complete. If your thoughts begin to drift, simply guide your attention back to your breath and to the truth of His presence. When your time concludes, reflect on what surfaced. Was it peace, discomfort, clarity, or conviction? Stillness often reveals what noise has been hiding.

- Schedule the time and treat it like a meeting
- Silence your phone and remove distractions.

Prayer

God, I'm so used to filling every moment. But today, I choose to be still. To quiet my thoughts, slow my pace, and simply be with You. Teach me to rest in Your presence, not just as a moment, but as a rhythm. Remind me that You are God, and that is enough. Amen.

Guide Your Thinking:

1. *What keeps me from practicing stillness regularly?*

2. *How might building a habit of stillness shift the way I think, pray, and live?*

DAY 6
Receiving God's Love
Before Earning It

Scripture

"But God demonstrates his own love for us in this: While we were still sinners, Christ died for us."

Romans 5:8 (NIV)

Reflection

Let us begin with what may feel like the most offensive idea in the gospel, which is that God loved you before you did a single thing right. This truth is not sentimental comfort but a divine disruption to the perfectionist within you, because deep down, many of us still believe love is awarded like a degree and earned through discipline, devotion, and visible growth.

You may have conditioned yourself to treat God like a divine employer rather than a Father by trading obedience for worth, effort for affection, and output for presence. Your grind for grace may reveal that you have forgotten grace was already given. You may resemble someone who keeps showing up spiritually, not because love feels secure, but because hope whispers that perhaps today you will finally be enough.

Although you would never say this out loud, your behavior often exposes it. You may feel more loved on the days you wake up early to pray, avoid God when you fail like a child hiding after breaking something valuable, and believe grace in theory while living as if you must earn your way back into favor.

Romans 5:8 makes it unmistakable that Christ did not die for a better version of you and that He did not wait for improvement. He died while you were still sinning, which means this is not poetic language but scandalous mercy. Earned love gives you control, but received love requires surrender. Earned love allows you to measure your value, but received love removes the scale entirely.

You do not climb toward grace because you fall into it. You do not achieve God's love because you collapse under it. God is not holding a clipboard; He is holding a cross, and that is enough. It has always been enough.

Application

Write this sentence and complete it honestly: "I still feel like I have to earn God's love when I _ _ _ _ _ _." Then read Romans 5:8 in full and read it aloud, not as a verse to memorize but as a verdict spoken over your life. Afterward, sit in silence for five minutes without offering explanation, apology, or performance, and allow yourself simply to be loved.

Prayer

God, I confess, grace unsettles me. I'd rather fix than receive. I'd rather prove than rest. But today I stop. No more deals. No more performance. You loved me at my worst. You love me now. Help me live like that's true. Amen.

Guide Your Thinking:

1. *What part of me still believes I need to "be better" before God will draw close?*

2. *How has spiritual performance shaped my view of God's love?*

3. *What would change if I lived from love instead of trying to earn it?*

_____

_____

_____

_____

_____

_____

_____

_____

_____

_____

_____

_____

_____

_____

_____

_____

_____

_____

_____

_____

DAY 7
The Call to Surrender

Scripture

"Whoever wants to be my disciple must deny themselves and take up their cross daily and follow me."

Luke 9:23 (NIV)

Reflection

Surrender. It's a word we often associate with defeat or loss. In the world's eyes, to surrender means to give up, to stop fighting, to lose ground, to relinquish control. But in the Kingdom of God, surrender is not defeat; it's the beginning of real freedom.

Jesus didn't say, "If you want to follow Me, bring your resume." He said, "Deny yourself. Take up your cross. Follow Me." That's the call. Not to a comfortable life, but to a crucified one. One where we willingly lay down the throne of our own desires and invite Jesus to take His rightful place as King.

That's hard, isn't it?

We like control. We like predictability. We like holding onto our timelines, expectations, and ideas of what "blessing" should look like. But Jesus is not asking for part of our lives. He's asking for everything. And not because He wants to take something from us, but because He wants to give us something better: Himself.

Surrender is not a punishment; it's a pathway. It's how we enter into peace, into purpose, into power. But it will cost you. It will cost you pride. It will cost you comfort. It might even cost you good things that once served you in one season but are now holding you back from what God wants to do in this one.

Ask Abraham. He laid his son on an altar. Ask Mary. She laid her reputation at the feet of a risky obedience. Ask Jesus. He laid His life down to do the will of the Father. And through their surrender, the world was changed.

What might God do through your surrender?

There is nothing you can surrender to Jesus that He will not redeem in His time. Nothing you release that He will not reshape for your good and His glory. But He won't force it. Surrender must be chosen daily, deliberately, even tearfully at times.

This isn't about striving. It's about trust. It's about loosening your grip and saying, "God, I believe You're better at leading my life than I am." That kind of surrender is where healing begins. It's where burdens lift. It's where striving ceases and real transformation begins.

So, what are you still holding?

Application

Take time today to identify one area where God is asking for deeper surrender. Is it a relationship? A habit? A dream? Control over your future?

Write it down honestly in a journal. Then, in prayer, speak it aloud as an offering: *"Lord, I surrender this to You."*

You may need to repeat this surrender tomorrow and the day after. That's okay. Surrender is not a one-time act. It's a lifestyle of trust.

Prayer

Jesus, I've held onto so many things, fears, dreams, plans, and pride. I confess how hard it is to let go. But I trust You. I trust that Your ways are higher, that Your love is perfect, and that You lead me with grace. Today, I choose to surrender, not out of fear, but out of faith. Teach me to walk open-handed, heart-first, and fully Yours. Amen.

Guide Your Thinking:

1. *What am I still trying to control that God is asking me to release?*

2. *How would my life look different if I lived from a place of full surrender?*

_____

_____

_____

_____

_____

_____

_____

_____

_____

_____

_____

_____

_____

_____

_____

_____

END OF WEEK 1
Laying The Foundation for Growth

You've completed the first week of this 60-day journey, and that's worth celebrating. Not because every moment was perfect, but because you chose to show up. You chose to seek Jesus even in the midst of your routines, doubts, and distractions. That choice matters. It speaks of a heart willing to grow.

This week wasn't just about doing devotionals; it was about planting roots. Deep ones. You've begun building a spiritual foundation that will sustain you far beyond these pages. Reflecting Christ's image, walking in humility, choosing joy in hardship, loving with intention, showing patience, offering forgiveness, and cultivating gratitude, these aren't simply nice ideas. They are transformative postures. They are counter-cultural and often costly. But they lead to freedom.

You may not see drastic changes yet. That's okay. Seeds take time. Growth often starts in hidden places beneath the surface of the ordinary. But God is at work in you, shaping your heart in ways you can't always measure.

And friend, He delights in every step you take toward Him. Every whispered prayer. Every small act of obedience. Every surrendered moment. None of it is wasted.

So, take a breath. Reflect. Celebrate. You're becoming. Not by striving but by surrendering. Not by perfection but by presence. The foundation you're laying now will carry you through future storms.

As you look ahead to Week 2, ask the Holy Spirit to keep tilling the soil of your heart. Stay open. Stay honest. Stay hungry for Him.

You are not walking alone.

Key Questions to Guide Your Thinking:

1. *What part of this week's journey stirred something deep within me?*

2. *Where did I resist, and what might God be inviting me to release?*

3. *What has surprised me about God's presence this week?*

4. *Write a prayer of thanksgiving and ask for grace to go deeper in the weeks to come.*

_____

_____

_____

_____

_____

_____

_____

_____

_____

_____

_____

_____

_____

_____

_____

_____

_____

_____

_____

_____

_____

_____

_____

_____

Journal

_____
_____
_____
_____
_____
_____
_____
_____
_____
_____
_____
_____
_____
_____
_____
_____
_____
_____
_____
_____
_____
_____
_____
_____
_____
_____
_____

WEEK 2

DAY 8
Anointed for the Ordinary, Finding God in the Daily

Scripture

"So whether you eat or drink or whatever you do, do it all for the glory of God."

1 Corinthians 10:31 (NIV)

Reflection

We often expect to meet God in big, mountaintop moments, at the altar, in breakthrough seasons, or during powerful worship. But most of life doesn't happen on mountaintops. Most of life is ordinary. Dishes. Deadlines. Driving. Repeating rhythms that feel anything but spiritual.

But what if the ordinary isn't a detour from your spiritual life, but *the place God most wants to meet you?*

Scripture is full of moments where God shows up in mundane spaces: Moses was tending sheep when he saw the burning bush. Ruth was gleaning leftovers in a field. Jesus spent 30 years in obscurity as a carpenter before ever performing a miracle. These aren't gaps in the story. They are the story.

God is not waiting for your next big breakthrough. He's walking with you now. In the laundry room. In the staff meeting. In the school drop-off line. In the way you respond to interruptions, in how you serve when no one claps, and in how you love when it's inconvenient.

The sacred isn't limited to Sunday. It's woven into every surrendered moment of your life.

The enemy would love for you to believe your life doesn't matter until it feels more significant. But the Kingdom of God grows in the soil of the ordinary. Faithfulness in unseen places is still anointed work. When you do it with love, with presence, with gratitude, it becomes holy ground.

You're not waiting to start your spiritual life when things slow down, get easier, or become more exciting. It's happening now. Right here. God is with you in the middle of your most normal day, and He delights in it. The way you sweep the floor, offer a smile, or finish a task with excellence can be worship. You were never meant to chase a platform to be significant. Your significance is already sealed in Him. He's not waiting for perfection. He's present in your participation. And that is more than enough.

Application

Choose one "ordinary" part of your day and make it sacred. That might mean folding laundry while praying over your family, commuting while worshiping, or turning meal prep into a moment of praise.

Notice what shifts when you do ordinary things with intentionality and worship.

Prayer

Lord, help me stop separating the sacred from the everyday. Teach me to find You in the quiet, the repetitive, the ordinary. Let my smallest moments be filled with Your presence. Anoint the mundane and show me the beauty of being faithful in things unseen. Amen.

Guide Your Thinking:

1. *Where have I been overlooking God's presence because something feels "too ordinary"?*

2. *How can I begin treating daily tasks as acts of worship?*

_____

_____

_____

_____

_____

_____

_____

_____

_____

DAY 9
Speaking Truth with Love

Scripture

"Instead, speaking the truth in love, we will grow to become in every respect the mature body of Him who is the head, that is, Christ."

Ephesians 4:15 (NIV)

Reflection

There's a distinct difference between being honest and being harsh. We've all experienced moments where truth was used more like a weapon than a tool for healing. Yet scripture teaches that truth should be paired with love, not to avoid hard conversations, but to make them redemptive.

Jesus modeled this perfectly. He never shied away from confronting sin, but He always did so with compassion. When He corrected the woman at the well or confronted Peter's denial, His words were full of grace, restoring rather than condemning.

Truth without love wounds; love without truth withholds growth. The goal of correction isn't to win an argument or feel righteous; it's to build others up, help them grow, and honor Christ in our relationships. As Paul reminds us in Colossians 4:6, our speech should always be gracious, seasoned with salt, bringing both flavor and preservation.

This applies deeply in our closest relationships: marriages, friendships, and workplaces, where truth is needed most and where it's easiest to speak from frustration. Speaking in love means we pause, pray, and examine our motives before we open our mouths. It means choosing humility over pride, restoration over retaliation.

Ask yourself: Am I using truth to heal or to hurt? Am I withholding the truth to keep peace at the cost of someone's growth? When we speak truth in love, we become instruments of God's transformation in the lives of others.

When we courageously speak with both conviction and compassion, we become a reflection of God's justice and mercy working in tandem. It's not about silencing ourselves or softening the truth. It's about anchoring it in love so it can heal, not harden. Truth becomes transformative when it's delivered from a surrendered heart.

Application

Think of one relationship where a loving truth needs to be shared, or where healing is needed after words were spoken too harshly. Before you speak, take time to pray, asking God for both clarity and gentleness. Write out what you want to say, and ask: "Does this reflect Jesus?"

If reconciliation is needed, take the first step. If a difficult conversation lies ahead, approach it with grace and the goal of growth, not victory. And if you've hurt someone with your words, humble yourself and make it right.

Prayer

Lord, teach me to speak the truth with love. Help me to use my words to build up others rather than hurt them. Give me the humility to correct people with kindness and wisdom to know when to speak, when to be quiet, and when to listen. Amen.

Guide Your Thinking:

1. *How can I balance truth and love in my conversations today?*

2. *Is there a conversation I need to revisit with more grace?*

_____

_____

_____

_____

_____

_____

_____

_____

_____

DAY 10
Resting in God's Presence

Scripture

"Come to me, all you who are weary and burdened, and I will give you rest."

Matthew 11:28 (NIV)

Reflection

We live in a world that celebrates hustle and rewards productivity. From the moment we wake up, we're bombarded with messages that say, *Do more. Be more. Prove more.* But in the midst of that noise, Jesus whispers something radically different: *"Come to Me... and I will give you rest."*

This isn't just a call to take a nap or schedule a weekend off. It's a sacred invitation to return to the very heart of who you are: a beloved child of God who is already enough, not because of what you've done, but because of who He is.

Jesus knows the burdens you carry, the internal pressures to perform, the hidden griefs that weigh you down, the relentless expectations you place on yourself. And He's not asking you to fix it all before coming to Him. He's asking you to bring it with you.

To rest in God's presence is to exhale. It's to stop running and striving and finally just be. It's allowing your soul to settle into His goodness, to lay your weary head on the shoulder of the One who never grows tired. It's remembering that your worth doesn't come from how much you achieve but from the God who knits you together and calls you His own.

This kind of rest doesn't ignore the realities of life; it strengthens you to face them. It resets your spirit. It silences the lies that say you're only as valuable as your performance. In His presence, you don't have to hold it all together. You just have to show up and let Him hold you.

You weren't created to live exhausted. You were created to abide. Rest is holy. Stillness is worship. Presence is power. And in Jesus, your soul will find the peace it's been craving.

Application

Set aside five to ten minutes today to be still with God. No agenda. Just be. Breathe deeply, pray simply, and listen quietly. Let this be a sacred pause where your heart meets His peace.

Notice moments when you feel rushed, stressed, or overwhelmed throughout your day. Use those moments to return to this promise: He will give you rest. Whisper a prayer of surrender and invite God to carry what you cannot.

Make this a habit, morning or evening, even for a few minutes. Build rhythm into your life that prioritizes presence over pressure, stillness over striving.

Prayer

Lord, I come to You weary and burdened. Teach me to rest in You, not just with my body, but with my heart and mind. Help me release control and trust Your love to carry me. Be my peace today. Amen.

Guide Your Thinking:

1. *What burdens am I carrying that God is inviting me to release?*

2. *How can I create space in my day for stillness and presence?*

_____

_____

_____

_____

_____

_____

_____

_____

_____

DAY 11
When God Says Wait, Worshipping in the Delay

Scripture

"I remain confident of this: I will see the goodness of the Lord in the land of the living. Wait for the Lord; be strong and take heart and wait for the Lord."

Psalm 27:13–14 (NIV)

Reflection

Waiting doesn't come naturally. We want clarity. Movement. Resolution. We want to know that God has heard us and that something is shifting. But sometimes, the answer is not a "yes" or "no," but a holy whisper: "Wait."

Waiting seasons can feel lonely and confusing. You pray, but heaven seems quiet. You obey, but the door remains closed. You believe, but nothing looks different.

And in that tension, the enemy will try to convince you that silence is absence, that God has forgotten, that your prayers didn't work, that nothing is happening.

But the truth is, the waiting is where some of God's deepest work happens.

Waiting is not punishment, it's preparation. It's where roots are formed. Where trust is tested. Where faith goes from theory to practice. God isn't just working on the outcome. He's working on you. From your perspective. Your posture. Your ability to hold the blessing without it crushing your soul.

David, who wrote this psalm, knew what it meant to wait. Anointed to be king but running for his life. Promised the throne, yet stuck in caves. And still he writes: *"I will see the goodness of the Lord."* That's not denial. That's *defiant hope*.

Worshipping in the wait doesn't mean pretending everything is fine. It means anchoring your heart in the truth that even here, even now, God is still worth it. He's still moving. He's still forming, so you're not stuck you're being still. And there's a difference. Stillness is not the absence of purpose; it's the posture of trust. In that quiet space, God is still speaking, shaping, and sanctifying. The enemy may call it delay, but heaven calls it development. Don't confuse silence for stagnation. You're in a sacred pause, and God is writing something beautiful in this waiting. You're not forgotten; you're being fortified.

So today, lift your hands even if they're tired. Whisper a prayer even if you feel numb. Sing even if the tears fall. Because every act of worship in the waiting shapes your soul to receive what's next.

Application

Write a letter to God about something you've been waiting on. Be honest, don't hold back frustration or longing. Then, take a moment to write a second letter: one of faith. Declare what you know is true about His character, even in the silence.

Choose one way to worship while you wait. It could be a song, a verse, or an act of generosity. Let that worship be your weapon against weariness.

Prayer

God, I don't always understand Your timing, but I trust Your heart. Teach me to wait well. To worship even when I don't see movement. To believe You're working beneath the surface of my life. Let the waiting shape me, not break me. And let my hope remain anchored in who You are. Amen.

Guide Your Thinking:

1. *What has waiting revealed about my faith and view of God?*

2. *How can I honor God now, even before the breakthrough comes?*

_____

_____

_____

_____

_____

_____

_____

_____

DAY 12
Living by Faith

Scripture

"Now faith is confidence in what we hope for and assurance about what we do not see."

Hebrews 11:1 (NIV)

Reflection

Living by faith sounds compelling until faith demands obedience without clarity. Faith becomes real when prayers seem unanswered, when obedience costs something tangible, and when God feels distant rather than nearby. Scripture defines faith not as emotion or certainty but as confidence in what we hope for and assurance about what we do not see. This definition requires trust that is rooted not in visible evidence but in the unchanging character of God.

Faith often requires stepping forward without knowing how the story will unfold. It calls you to remain obedient when outcomes are unclear and to continue trusting when circumstances suggest retreat. Many of us want a blueprint before we move, but faith invites us to move because we trust the One who holds the blueprint. It requires surrendering the demand for proof and accepting that obedience may precede understanding.

The men and women described in Hebrews chapter eleven were not shielded from delay or suffering. Abraham followed God without knowing his destination. Moses led people who frequently resisted him. Rahab risked her life based on what she believed about God's power. Some of these individuals did not see the full fulfillment of the promises made in their lifetimes, yet they remained faithful. Their lives testify that faith is not validated by immediate results but by persistent trust.

Faith does not deny pain or pretend uncertainty does not exist. It chooses obedience in the presence of uncertainty and rests in the assurance that God is faithful even when circumstances are unstable. When you forgive without guaranteed reconciliation, continue praying without visible change, or remain obedient despite confusion, you are practicing durable faith. Such faith is not built on outcomes but on who God is. Even when your understanding is limited, His character remains constant and worthy of trust.

Application

Name the place in your life where faith feels most irrational right now and speak it aloud. Then say that even here God is still God. Take one action today that requires trust, whether it is forgiving, apologizing, risking, or obeying without visible confirmation. Choose presence over proof.

Prayer

God, I want to trust You, but I also want proof. I want guarantees. Maps. Milestones. But You've never operated that way. So today, I choose obedience over answers. I choose presence over clarity. I choose You. Even here. Even now. Even if. Amen.

Guide Your Thinking:

1. *What part of my life am I waiting to see "work out" before I fully trust God?*

2. *Is my faith built on outcomes, or on who God is, regardless of what He does?*

_____

_____

_____

_____

_____

_____

_____

_____

_____

DAY 13
Guarding Your Thoughts

Scripture

"We take captive every thought to make it obedient to Christ."

2 Corinthians 10:5 (NIV)

Reflection

Our thoughts shape our lives more than we realize. What we dwell on influences our emotions, our choices, and even our spiritual growth. That's why scripture calls us not just to monitor our thoughts, but to take them captive and align them with Christ.

A pastor once shared his early struggle with lust and destructive habits. It all began, he said, with seemingly harmless choices: what he watched, who he spent time with, and what music he listened to. Over time, those influences shaped his thinking, then his desires, and eventually his behavior. The battle wasn't just external; it was rooted in his mind.

We all experience mental patterns that need re-aligning: fear, comparison, resentment, and insecurity. If left unchecked, they can distort our view of God, ourselves, and others. But here's the hope: we are not powerless. Through Christ, we have the authority to interrupt toxic thought patterns and replace them with truth.

Taking thoughts captive is not about ignoring reality or suppressing emotion, it's about replacing lies with God's Word. It's choosing to meditate on what is true, noble, right, pure, and lovely (Philippians 4:8), rather than what is anxious, bitter, or unkind.

This kind of mental discipline takes time, but it transforms us from the inside out. When our thoughts are ruled by Christ, our lives begin to reflect His peace, power, and purpose.

Our minds are battlefields, and what we allow to dwell there ultimately determines the course of our lives. Every thought has the potential to either strengthen our walk with Christ or pull us further from it. That's why Scripture doesn't simply tell us to avoid bad thoughts; it tells us to take them captive to make them obedient to Christ (2 Corinthians 10:5). This is the language of war, not passivity. It implies that we must be vigilant, active, and discerning in our mental life.

Thoughts may come uninvited, but they don't have to stay unchallenged. Whether it's the internal echo of insecurity, the lie that says you're not enough, or the temptation that creeps in through exhaustion, each thought presents a moment of choice. Will we let it take root, or will we hold it up to the truth of Christ?

Renewing our minds is not a one-time event. It's a daily discipline. And it begins with awareness. Too often, we live on mental auto-pilot, unaware of the narratives we've allowed to repeat for years. But transformation comes when we interrupt those loops and speak life into the spaces where darkness has lingered.

This is more than positive thinking; it's Spirit-led renewal. When we align our thoughts with God's truth, peace replaces anxiety, confidence displaces fear, and joy rises where despair once lived. You don't have to believe everything you think. And you don't have to fight this battle alone. The Spirit of God empowers you to choose what you meditate on, and He will train your heart to recognize His voice over every lie.

Your thoughts shape your world. So, make them a place where Christ is welcomed. Where grace is louder than guilt, hope stronger than despair, and truth more familiar than fear.

Application

Be intentional today about your mental input. Pay attention to recurring thoughts especially those that cause fear, anger, shame, or doubt. Ask yourself: *Is this thought aligned with God's truth?*

Write down one harmful thought and find a Scripture that counters it. Speak that verse aloud throughout the day. Repeat this as often as needed, this is how you train your mind in truth.

Create a habit of pausing during anxious or tempting moments to ask: *"Is this helping me become more like Christ?"* Over time, those pauses become pathways to peace.

Prayer

Lord, renew my mind. Help me recognize the thoughts that are not from You and give me the strength to replace them with Your truth. Let my mind be a reflection of Your Spirit at work within me. Amen.

Guide Your Thinking:

1. *What recurring thoughts do I need to surrender to God today?*

2. *How can I build a habit of thinking on things that are true and life-giving?*

_____

_____

_____

_____

_____

_____

_____

_____

_____

_____

_____

_____

_____

_____

_____

_____

_____

_____

_____

_____

_____

DAY 14
Pursuing Peace

Scripture

"Blessed are the peacemakers, for they will be called children of God."

Matthew 5:9 (NIV)

Reflection

The world is longing for peace, but not just peace in the abstract. We long for peace in our homes, in our minds, in our relationships. Yet, if we're honest, peace often feels more like a distant dream than a present reality. Conflict dominates headlines, but it also festers in the quiet corners of our lives, silent grudges, broken friendships, unspoken wounds.

Jesus doesn't just call us to live in peace; He calls us to make peace. That's not the same as avoiding conflict. Being a peacemaker means stepping into tension with courage, humility, and love, choosing restoration over retaliation. It means creating space for healing, even when it's uncomfortable or undeserved.

Peace starts within. If we're filled with anxiety, bitterness, or unresolved anger, it's nearly impossible to bring peace to others. That's why scripture reminds us that Christ Himself is our peace (Ephesians 2:14). Before we can be peacemakers, we must first become peace-receivers, anchoring our hearts in God's presence and learning to trust His voice above the noise.

Look at Jesus: in the middle of a violent storm, He slept. Not because the storm wasn't real, but because His peace wasn't dependent on circumstances. As His followers, we're called to carry that same peace into every room, every conversation, every disagreement.

Being a peacemaker doesn't mean keeping everyone happy; it means choosing what brings wholeness. It means forgiving first, listening well, and laying down pride. It might mean breaking the silence with a hard but healing word, or offering grace when you'd rather walk away.

You don't need a title or platform to be a peacemaker. All you need is a surrendered heart, willing to reflect the Prince of Peace in a world that desperately needs Him.

Application

Start by inviting God's peace into your own heart. Spend five minutes in silence today, no music, no distractions. Just you and God. Ask Him, "Where am I lacking peace?" Listen. Let His Spirit show you what you need to surrender, fear, resentment, and control.

Next, ask: Who do I need to bring peace to? It could be someone you've avoided, someone you've hurt, or someone who hurt you. Pray for them by name. Then, take one step, send a message, initiate a conversation, or simply commit to responding in love the next time tension rises.

Let your life be a ripple of peace, wherever you go, may others encounter Christ through your calm, your courage, and your grace.

Prayer

Jesus, You are the Prince of Peace. I invite Your peace into my heart today. Quiet my anxious thoughts and soften my hard places. Show me where I need to bring peace, and give me the boldness to be a vessel of Your healing love. Use me to build bridges where there are walls. Amen.

Guide Your Thinking:

1. *What is one area in my life where I need to receive God's peace more fully?*

2. *Who in my life needs peace, and how might God use me to bring it to them?*

_____

_____

_____

_____

_____

_____

_____

_____

END OF WEEK 2
Embracing God's Process

You've reached the end of your second week, and that's no small accomplishment. These past 14 days have invited you into a rhythm of reflection, surrender, and transformation. Whether every day felt impactful or some felt quiet, trust this: God is doing deep work in you.

This week focused on growing in foundational habits of the heart: patience, forgiveness, gratitude, surrender, faith, mental renewal, and peace. Each one may have stretched you in different ways, but together, they are preparing the soil for something beautiful.

Think about Joseph. Before he saw his dreams fulfilled, he endured betrayal, slavery, and prison. On the surface, it may have looked like delay or even failure, but beneath it all, God was shaping his character, strengthening his faith, and setting the stage for a much greater purpose.

The same is true for you. You may not always see immediate results. Some prayers might still feel unanswered. But the process matters. Your willingness to keep showing up, to pray, reflect, trust, and take small steps of obedience, is proof that God is growing something eternal in you.

So, pause now. Celebrate what God has begun. Let gratitude rise for what He's already revealed. And take heart in knowing this: transformation doesn't happen in a single moment, it unfolds as we walk with Him, one day at a time.

Key Questions to Guide Your Thinking:

1. *What has God revealed about Himself, or about me, during these last two weeks?*

2. *Where have I resisted the process? What would it look like to surrender that part of my heart?*

3. *What habit or truth has encouraged or challenged me most so far?*

4. *Write a prayer of gratitude, acknowledging the work God is doing, even in unseen places.*

_____

_____

_____

_____

_____

_____

_____

_____

_____

_____

_____

_____

_____

_____

_____

Journal

_____
_____
_____
_____
_____
_____
_____
_____
_____
_____
_____
_____
_____
_____
_____
_____
_____
_____
_____
_____
_____
_____
_____
_____

WEEK 3

DAY 15
Practicing Generosity

Scripture

"Each of you should give what you have decided in your heart to give, not reluctantly or under compulsion, for God loves a cheerful giver."

2 Corinthians 9:7 (NIV)

Reflection

In 2016, Brenda Jones, a 69-year-old woman from Texas, had been waiting over a year for a liver transplant. When the call finally came, she learned that a critically ill 23-year-old woman named Abigail also needed that very organ to survive. Without hesitation, Brenda gave up her place on the transplant list, saving Abigail's life. Miraculously, another liver became available for Brenda just days later, and she, too, recovered fully. Her story is a stunning portrait of cheerful, sacrificial generosity.

True generosity flows from a heart that trusts God to provide, not just financially, but in every area of life. It's not limited to money; it includes our time, energy, encouragement, forgiveness, and attention. When we give cheerfully, we echo the very heart of God, who gave us everything, even His Son.

Jesus never gave with strings attached. He gave because love compelled Him to. His life was a continuous outpouring: healing, teaching, feeding, forgiving, and ultimately giving His life for us. As we grow in Christ, our hearts are shaped to give freely, not from guilt, but from grace.

Generosity isn't about how much you have; it's about what you're willing to release. It's about recognizing that everything you've been given, whether a talent, a dollar, or a spare hour, is a tool in God's hands to bless others.

Living generously transforms more than just those around us; it softens our hearts, opens our eyes to others' needs, and reminds us of how much we've received. It's a powerful act of faith that says, "God, I trust You to fill what I pour out."

And perhaps most importantly, generosity anchors us in eternity. Every act of giving, no matter how small, plants a seed that outlives us. Whether it's encouraging a weary soul, serving someone unseen, or sharing resources with those in need, generosity becomes a living testimony of God's love on display.

When we give joyfully, we don't just meet needs, we mirror the gospel. We reflect the radical, undeserved grace we've received. And in a world marked by scarcity mindsets, fear, and self-preservation, cheerful giving is a revolutionary act of faith. It declares that our security doesn't come from what we keep but from the One who never stops giving.

Application

Ask God to show you one specific way to practice generosity today. It might be financial, but it could also be your time, a word of encouragement, an unexpected favor, or simply slowing down to truly listen to someone.

Give freely, without expectation, without recognition. Then reflect: how did it feel to give? What did it reveal about your relationship with what you have and with the God who gave it?

Look for ways to make generosity a rhythm, not just a reaction. Consider starting a weekly "generosity habit", something small but consistent that keeps your heart open and your hands willing.

Prayer

Father, thank You for all You've given me, Your love, Your grace, and every blessing in my life. Help me hold nothing too tightly. Teach me to give joyfully and freely, trusting that You'll meet every need. Use my generosity to reflect Your heart.
Amen.

Guide Your Thinking:

1. *What do I have today that someone else might need?*

2. *What holds me back from giving freely, and how can I surrender that to God?*

_____

_____

_____

_____

_____

_____

_____

_____

_____

DAY 16
Living by Obedience

Scripture

"If you love me, you will keep my commands."

John 14:15 (ESV)

Reflection

Obedience is one of the most challenging and misunderstood aspects of the Christian walk. In a world that celebrates autonomy, self-expression, and doing what "feels right," obedience can seem outdated or even oppressive. But in the Kingdom of God, obedience is not about legalism; it's about love.

Jesus didn't say, "If you fear me, obey me." He said, "If you love me, keep my commands." Obedience is the natural response of a heart captured by grace. It's what happens when we trust that God's ways are not only higher, but better.

Look at Noah. He obeyed God's call to build an ark despite years of ridicule and no visible reason to prepare for a flood. Or Abraham, who left behind everything familiar because of a promise. Mary surrendered her body, her reputation, and her future to carry the Son of God. None of them knew exactly how their story would unfold, but they obeyed, and through their obedience, God's purposes were fulfilled.

Obedience is rarely easy. It may ask you to forgive when you'd rather hold a grudge, to step into something unknown when you'd prefer to stay where it's comfortable or to remain faithful in a season that feels silent. It often means surrendering control and choosing trust over understanding.

Yet, here's the beautiful truth: obedience invites God's presence into your life in powerful ways. Every time you say yes to God, whether in something large or small, you create space for Him to move. You begin to live with clarity, confidence, and peace, even when circumstances don't change immediately.

Disobedience often disguises itself as delay. "I'll do it later." "I'm just waiting for confirmation." But delayed obedience is still disobedience. God isn't waiting for you to be perfect. He's waiting for your response. Sometimes, the next breakthrough in your journey won't come from more prayer or more planning, but from simply taking the next obedient step.

Application

Start by asking this simple, bold question: "Lord, where am I resisting You?" Be honest. Write down whatever comes to mind, a relationship, a habit, a decision, a place where fear has held you back.

Then, take action. Obedience doesn't have to be dramatic. It might mean apologizing to someone, starting something God's put on your heart, letting go of control in a specific area, or simply being faithful in a task that feels unseen.

Write a short prayer of surrender, and if you're journaling, list out the "yeses" you've given to God lately. Let this be a testimony of your faith in motion.

Prayer

Lord, thank You for calling me not just to believe in You, but to follow You. I confess the areas where I've hesitated, where fear or pride has held me back. Today, I choose obedience, not because I have all the answers, but because I trust Your heart. Teach me to walk in step with You. Amen.

Guide Your Thinking:

1. *What is one step of obedience I've been avoiding, and what's holding me back?*

2. *How might my obedience open the door for God to work in my life or be in some-one else's?*

_____

_____

_____

_____

_____

_____

_____

_____

_____

DAY 17
Releasing Control

Scripture

"Trust in the Lord with all your heart and lean not on your own understanding; in all your ways submit to him, and he will make your paths straight."

Proverbs 3:5–6 (NIV)

Reflection

We like control because it makes us feel safe. It gives the illusion that we can manage outcomes, protect ourselves from pain, and guarantee success. But control is often a spiritual mirage, something we chase, only to find it slipping through our fingers.

God doesn't call us to live tightly gripped lives. He calls us to live open-handed, surrendered, and free. That freedom begins when we admit: *"I'm not in control, and that's okay."*

Think of Moses. When God called him to lead Israel, Moses panicked: "What if they don't listen? What if I'm not enough?" His desire for control clashed with God's invitation to trust. Yet when Moses finally let go, God's power was released through him in ways he never imagined.

Releasing control isn't weakness, its strength rooted in faith. It's saying, "God, You know more than I do. I'm tired of trying to orchestrate everything. I trust Your plan even when I don't understand it."

Sometimes, control shows up subtly, in our need to fix people, manage every detail, or avoid risk. Other times, it shows up in fear, fear of the unknown, fear of being hurt, fear that God won't come through. But every time we release control, we make space for God to move, to lead, and to carry what was never ours to bear.

Letting go doesn't mean doing nothing. It means doing your part and trusting God with the rest. It's praying, obeying, and then releasing the outcome into His hands.

But here's the challenge: surrender rarely feels safe in the moment. It often feels like loss, like weakness, like failure. Yet every story of true spiritual strength begins with surrender. Control may offer short-term comfort, but it will never produce lasting peace. Peace is found in trusting a sovereign God whose hands are far more capable than our own.

Even Jesus, in the Garden of Gethsemane, wrestled with the weight of surrender. "Not my will, but Yours be done," He prayed. And in that prayer, power was released. The redemption of the world began not at the cross, but in the moment Jesus released control.

That's our model. That's our invitation, not to live in fear or self-reliance but to live in the freedom that comes from trusting the One who holds every detail of our story.

Application

Today, identify one area where you're holding on too tightly. Maybe it's a relationship, a financial situation, a future decision, or a personal goal. Write it down. Then, symbolically open your hands as you pray: "Lord, I give this to You."

Throughout the day, when anxiety rises or the need to control kicks in, pause. Breathe. Remind yourself: "God is in control, and He is good." Speak Proverbs 3:5–6 aloud as a declaration of trust.

Repeat this act of surrender daily if needed. Over time, you'll feel the freedom that comes not from controlling everything, but from being held by the One who controls it all.

Prayer

God, I've tried to carry things that were never mine to hold. I surrender my plans, my fears, and my desire for control. Help me trust You more deeply each day. Let Your peace rule my heart and guide me step by step as I follow You. Amen.

Guide Your Thinking:

1. *What area of my life am I trying to control right now?*

2. *How does trusting God change the way I respond to uncertainty?*

_____

_____

_____

_____

_____

_____

_____

_____

_____

_____

_____

_____

DAY 18
The Power of Words

Scripture

"The tongue has the power of life and death, and those who love it will eat its fruit."

Proverbs 18:21 (NIV)

Reflection

We often pretend our words are neutral, but they are not. Words are not weightless, and every sentence spoken carries influence. According to Scripture, every word has the potential to produce life or death, healing or harm. We may minimize careless speech as honesty or dismiss sarcasm as humor, but speech shapes souls, relationships, reputations, and even spiritual environments.

Consider how many of your defining memories involve language. Someone's affirmation may have strengthened your confidence, while someone's criticism may still echo in your thoughts. Words linger long after they are spoken because they imprint the heart. They create narratives that people carry for years. A single sentence can build a future or fracture trust.

Many of us have said words we wish we could take back. We have humiliated others, wounded trust, and disguised cruelty as truth. Emotional collapse and spiritual corrosion often begin with language. At the same time, words can resurrect what was dying. A sincere apology can mend division. Encouragement can restore courage. Truth spoken in love can redirect a life that was drifting.

Speech reveals the condition of the heart because what overflows from the mouth reflects what resides within. When pride, insecurity, or anger governs the heart, the tongue becomes destructive. When humility and surrender govern the heart, speech becomes constructive. The goal is not silence but sanctified speech that reflects the Spirit's influence.

You do not need a large audience to wield significant impact. Your words shape your home, your friendships, your workplace, and your spiritual influence. The question is not whether you possess power in your speech but how you will steward it. When surrendered to God, your voice becomes an instrument of restoration rather than reaction.

Application

Think of the last time your words caused harm, and name it honestly, without excuses or spiritual language to soften it. Ask God what needs to be rebuilt that your mouth damaged. Then choose one intentional act of speech today that costs you something, whether it is an apology, encouragement, or truth spoken with gentleness.

Prayer

God, forgive me for weaponizing my voice. For speaking before I prayed. For cutting people down with tone, not just truth. Train my tongue in resurrection, not reaction. Let my words be mirrors of You, not masks for my flesh. Amen.

Guide Your Thinking:

1. *Who has been most shaped by my words, for better or worse?*

2. *Where has silence been just as damaging as what I've said?*

_____

_____

_____

_____

_____

_____

_____

_____

DAY 19
Choosing Contentment

Scripture

"I have learned the secret of being content in any and every situation... I can do all this through him who gives me strength."

Philippians 4:12–13 (NIV)

Reflection

We live in a world built on upgrades. Advertisements constantly suggest we could be happier, thinner, wealthier, or more fulfilled, if only we had this. Social media feeds us filtered images of others' best moments, subtly whispering, "You're missing out." It's no wonder contentment feels so elusive.

But biblical contentment isn't about pretending everything is perfect. It's about choosing peace in the present, even when life doesn't match our plans.

Paul wrote these words about contentment not from a beachside retreat but from a prison cell. He wasn't immune to hunger, disappointment, or hardship, but he had learned a secret: true contentment doesn't come from getting everything you want; it comes from realizing that in Christ, you already have everything you need.

This kind of contentment is not passive resignation. It's a resilient trust, a declaration that *God's presence is enough, even when provi-*

sion hasn't come yet. It's choosing to be grateful for what you have, rather than being paralyzed by what you don't.

And this is something we learn. Paul says, "I have learned the secret..." That means contentment doesn't come naturally; it's a discipline. It's something we grow into as we walk closely with Christ, trust His provision, and resist the constant pull of comparison and entitlement.

Contentment frees you. It frees you from chasing what you think will finally make you happy. It frees you to enjoy your season, your calling, your people, and your portion without resentment. It allows you to stop measuring your life by someone else's highlight reel and start living fully in the grace you've already received.

Ultimately, contentment is a posture of the heart that says: *"If all I have is Jesus, I have enough."*

And it's often in the waiting that contentment is most deeply formed. When dreams delay, or prayers seem unanswered, contentment whispers: "Even this can still be holy." It's not about denial, it's about devotion. It's choosing to worship God, not just when He gives what you want, but because He is what you want. Contentment shifts the focus from lack to Lordship. It's about saying, "God, You are enough for me, even here, even now."

The world may tell you contentment is settling. But in the Kingdom, it's sacred. It's a bold act of trust to rest in the sufficiency of Christ when everything around you demands more. And when you do, you'll find a joy that isn't fragile, a peace that isn't shallow, and a confidence that doesn't require constant affirmation.

Application

Spend time today identifying where discontentment might be lurking. Is it in your finances, your relationships, your career, your body, or even your timeline?

Write a list of ten specific things you are grateful for, things you often overlook. Then, choose one area of discontentment and speak gratitude directly into it. For example, if you're discontent with your job, thank God for provision, growth, or the people it's brought into your life.

As you go through your day, catch yourself in moments of complaint or comparison. Redirect those thoughts with this truth: *"God is enough. What He's given me today is enough."*

Prayer

Lord, help me find joy in what I already have. Teach me to see Your goodness even in seasons of waiting or lack. Guard my heart from envy and comparison and fill it with gratitude. I trust that Your grace is sufficient for today, and every day to come. Amen.

Guide Your Thinking:

1. *How can practicing gratitude help me retain my heart toward contentment?*

2. *What area of my life fees "not enough" right now?*

_____

_____

_____

_____

_____

_____

_____

_____

_____

DAY 20
Living with Integrity

Scripture

"The righteous lead blameless lives; blessed are their children after them."

Proverbs 20:7 (NIV)

Reflection

Integrity is often quiet. It doesn't demand attention or applause. But over time, it speaks louder than charisma or talent ever could. It's the unseen decisions, the honest moment when lying would be easier, the quiet apology when no one expected one, the choice to do what's right when compromise is more convenient.

In today's world, image is everything. Social media allows us to curate a version of ourselves we want others to see. But God is not impressed by your image. He looks at the heart. And He honors those who walk in integrity, even when no one else notices.

Daniel's story reminds us that integrity isn't circumstantial; it's a conviction. Though taken captive in a foreign land, surrounded by corruption and idolatry, he remained faithful to God in both public influence and private devotion. His unwavering character was so consistent that even his enemies couldn't find fault in him, except in his commitment to prayer. Integrity isn't about perfection; it's about consistency. It's about refusing to compartmentalize our faith.

What about us? Are we the same people in private as we are in public? Are we honest with ourselves, with God, and with others, even when it costs us? Integrity requires courage, to admit when we're wrong, to say no to things that others say yes to, and to live by convictions rather than convenience.

But here's the promise: integrity is never wasted. It builds trust, strengthens relationships, and becomes a legacy. As Proverbs 20:7 reminds us, a righteous life leaves a blessing for the next generation. Your choices today don't just shape your story; they shape the spiritual atmosphere of your home, your community, and your lineage.

You don't have to be perfect. But you are called to be authentic. And when your life is anchored in integrity, you'll find a peace that pretense can never give.

Application

Take a moment to examine your "hidden life", the thoughts, habits, and choices that no one sees. Is there any area where your walk doesn't match your talk? Invite God to search your heart and reveal what needs to shift.

Consider one practical step you can take today to align your private and public life. That could mean setting boundaries around what you watch, speaking the truth in a situation where you've been silent, or confessing something that's lingered in the dark.

Also, ask yourself: What kind of example am I setting for those who follow me, children, peers, friends? Integrity multiplies when it's modeled.

Prayer

Father, I want to be a person of integrity. Help me align my private life with Your truth. Give me the courage to live honestly and humbly, even when it's hard. May my choices today reflect Your character, and may my life bring honor to You in every unseen moment. Amen.

Guide Your Thinking:

1. *Where in my life am I tempted to compromise for convenience or appearance?*

2. *What does it mean for me to walk in integrity today, practically and spiritually?*

_____

_____

_____

_____

_____

_____

_____

_____

_____

DAY 21
Cultivating Wisdom

Scripture

"The fear of the Lord is the beginning of wisdom, and knowledge of the Holy One is understanding."

Proverbs 9:10 (NIV)

Reflection

Wisdom is not simply the accumulation of knowledge but the ability to apply knowledge rightly. A person may possess information and still lack discernment, maturity, and spiritual clarity. Knowledge fills the mind, but wisdom shapes judgment and directs action. It is formed through experience, humility, and reverence for God. Wisdom listens carefully before speaking and pauses thoughtfully before reacting. It evaluates not only what is possible, but what is right.

Many people make decisions based on impulse, emotion, or personal preference. Wisdom, however, requires restraint and reflection. It seeks understanding before forming conclusions and pursues truth before defending a position. It recognizes that not every opportunity should be accepted and that not every opinion needs to be expressed. Wisdom considers long-term consequences rather than immediate gratification and values integrity over approval.

The book of Proverbs teaches that wisdom begins with the fear of the Lord, which means that wisdom grows out of a relationship with God. When we revere Him, we begin to see life through His perspective. Our choices become less about personal gain and more about faithful stewardship. We ask not only what benefits us but what honors Him. Wisdom allows us to navigate complexity without compromising conviction.

Cultivating wisdom requires intentional pursuit. It develops when we remain teachable, invite correction, and admit when we do not have all the answers. It deepens when we pause to pray before deciding and when we seek counsel from those who are spiritually mature. Over time, wisdom produces stability, clarity, and quiet confidence because it is anchored in truth rather than impulse. A wise life may not always be the loudest or most celebrated, but it is steady.

Application

Ask God specifically for wisdom in one decision you are currently facing. Write down the options before you and consider which choice most aligns with Scripture and reflects humility and obedience. Seek counsel from someone spiritually mature and remain open to guidance that challenges your assumptions.

Prayer

God, I've confused being clever with being wise. I've used knowledge to control, not to love. Dismantle my pride. Unseat my self-reliance. Give me a wisdom that's not loud, but holy, the kind that changes people, not just opinions. Amen.

Guide Your Thinking:

1. *Where in my life am I leaning on my own understanding rather than God's wisdom?*

2. *What would it look like to pursue wisdom more intentionally this week?*

_____

_____

_____

_____

_____

_____

_____

_____

_____

_____

_____

_____

_____

_____

_____

_____

_____

_____

_____

END OF WEEK 3
Midpoint Reflection - Building the Inner Life

You've just completed the third week,21 days of showing up, pressing in, and allowing God to shape you from the inside out. That's worth celebrating.

This week focused on what happens beneath the surface: obedience, surrender, integrity, and wisdom. These aren't just spiritual ideals; they're building blocks of a deep and anchored life in Christ. While others may focus on appearances, God is building something deeper in you: character, discernment, resilience, and faith that lasts.

Think of your heart as a house. Each reflection, prayer, and obedient choice this week has helped renovate the interior, tearing down what's not from Him and rebuilding with truth, grace, and strength. You may not feel the change instantly, but trust this: the inner work always shows up in time. What God builds in secret, He will use in the open.

Jesus said the wise builder is the one who hears His words and puts them into practice (Matthew 7:24). That's what you've been doing. And you're laying a foundation that will stand through any storm.

Pause now and take inventory. What's shifted in your heart this week? What conviction, truth, or practice stood out most? Where do you still sense resistance, and what would it look like to surrender that place to God?

Let these last three weeks fuel your hunger for what's ahead. You're not just reading devotionals; you're becoming someone different. Someone formed in the presence of God.

Key Questions to Guide Your Thinking:

1. *How has God been shaping and strengthening my faith over the past three weeks?*

2. *What habits, fears, or distractions is He inviting me to release so I can grow closer to Him?*

3. *What is one powerful truth or lesson that has resonated deeply with me during this journey?*

_____

_____

_____

_____

_____

_____

_____

_____

_____

_____

Journal

WEEK 4

DAY 22
Living a Life of Honor

Scripture

"Be devoted to one another in love. Honor one another above yourselves."

Romans 12:10 (NIV)

Reflection

Honor is a language of the Kingdom, but it's often forgotten in a world obsessed with self. To honor someone means to treat them as valuable, not because they've earned it, but because God says they are. It's about seeing people through the eyes of heaven, not through the lens of merit, status, or behavior.

In Romans 12, Paul urges believers to "honor one another above yourselves." This isn't about flattery or people-pleasing; it's about choosing humility, respect, and dignity in our interactions. It's speaking to the worth in others, even when their actions fall short of it.

Jesus lived a life of honor. He honored the Samaritan woman by speaking to her as an equal. He honored Zacchaeus by dining in his home. He honored children, the sick, and even His executioners, saying, "Father, forgive them." His honor wasn't conditional. It flowed from love.

A life of honor starts in the heart. It looks like holding your tongue instead of gossiping. Choosing compassion instead of judgment. Defending someone who can't repay you. Listening to someone whom others overlook. Honor isn't earned; it's given.

And honor has a ripple effect. When you elevate others, you create a culture where people feel safe, seen, and valued. Your family, friendships, workplace, and church become places where dignity is protected, and God's presence is welcome.

To live with honor is to live counter-culturally. It's to lower yourself to lift others up, not just in public, but especially in private. And in doing so, you reflect the heart of Christ.

But honor isn't just about how we treat others; it's also about how we respond to God. When we live with reverence for Him, we carry that same reverence into how we steward our words, time, relationships, and influence. We don't cut corners or act carelessly; we live with intention, knowing our lives reflect the One we serve.

Honoring others means we stop labeling people based on their past and start seeing them through the potential God placed within them. It's choosing to bless when we could criticize, to affirm when we could tear down, and to protect someone's dignity even when no one's watching.

In a world that's quick to dishonor, through sarcasm, judgment, and pride, those who walk in honor shine like lights. They become a safe presence in a harsh world. And that presence often speaks louder than any sermon.

Application

Ask God to show you someone who needs to be honored today, not for what they've done, but for who they are. This could be a family member you've taken for granted, a coworker who's overlooked, or even someone who's hurt you.

Take one step: speak encouragement, show appreciation, give time, or simply listen. Make it personal and sincere.

Also, reflect: Are there places where dishonor has crept in, criticism, sarcasm, or indifference? Invite God to purify your heart and speech and choose to speak life instead.

Prayer

Lord, help me live a life of honor. Teach me to see others as You do, to speak words that build and not break, and to elevate those around me. Let my life reflect the dignity of Your Kingdom and the humility of Your Son. Amen.

Guide Your Thinking:

1. *Who have I been treating as ordinary when God sees them as extraordinary?*

2. *What changes when I choose to honor others above myself?*

_____

_____

_____

_____

_____

_____

_____

_____

DAY 23
Enduring with Hope

Scripture

"Let us hold unswervingly to the hope we profess, for he who promised is faithful."

Hebrews 10:23 (NIV)

Reflection

Hope is often mistaken for naive optimism, a fragile feeling that things will somehow work out. But biblical hope is far more robust. It's not anchored in changing circumstances but in the unchanging nature of God. It's the confident expectation that God will keep His word, even when everything around us suggests otherwise.

Enduring hope is gritty. It shows up in the middle of heartache and says, "God is still good." It clings to truth when emotions waver. It remains when answers don't come quickly, when prayers feel unanswered, and when life is more questions than clarity.

Throughout scripture, we see this kind of hope lived out in the lives of the faithful. Abraham hoped against hope, believing God's promise even when his body and Sarah's womb were as good as dead. Job declared, "Though he slay me, yet will I hope in him." Jeremiah, in the middle of devastation, wrote, "Yet this I call to mind and therefore I have hope: because of the Lord's great love we are not consumed." (Lamentations 3:21–22)

What gave them this kind of enduring strength? It wasn't willpower. It was a matter of trusting in the faithfulness of God.

Hope is not the absence of pain; it's the refusal to let pain have the final word. It is the spiritual stamina to stay rooted when you feel like running, to keep sowing even when you haven't seen a harvest, and to keep praising even when you're still in the valley.

There will be moments when you feel worn down by the wait, whether you're waiting for healing, restoration, direction, or relief. The delay can feel like denial. But Scripture reminds us that those who wait on the Lord will renew their strength (Isaiah 40:31). While you're waiting, God is weaving something deeper into you: resilience, perspective, and dependence on Him.

Don't let discouragement become your default. Let hope become your discipline. Not a fleeting feeling, but a daily decision to believe that God is who He says He is, and that He will finish what He started.

Application

Take inventory of your heart today. Where have you grown weary in waiting? Be honest with God. Write it down, naming both the hope you're holding onto and the discouragement you've felt.

Then, spend a few minutes meditating on a scripture about hope, like Romans 5:3–5 or Psalm 27:13–14. Let God's Word strengthen what feels weak.

Do something today that reinforces your hope: worship, serve someone else, or revisit a journal entry of a past breakthrough. Let your actions declare that your faith isn't fading, it's being fortified.

Prayer

Lord, I confess that I get tired of waiting. Sometimes, my hope feels fragile. But today, I choose to anchor my soul in Your faithfulness. Remind me that You are never late and never absent. Help me endure with trust, knowing You are work-ing even when I can't see it. Let my hope in You be steadfast and strong. Amen.

Guide Your Thinking:

1.   *Where have I lost sight of hope in my current season?*

2.   *What does enduring faith look like for me today, practically and spiritually?*

_____

_____

_____

_____

_____

_____

_____

_____

_____

DAY 24
Embracing Grace

Scripture

"But he said to me, 'My grace is sufficient for you, for my power is made perfect in weakness.' Therefore I will boast all the more gladly about my weaknesses, so that Christ's power may rest on me."

2 Corinthians 12:9 (NIV)

Reflection

Grace is the undeserved, unearned, and unlimited favor of God, and yet, it's one of the most difficult gifts to truly embrace. We are often much more comfortable striving than receiving. We try to earn what has already been freely given, or we disqualify ourselves because we feel too broken, too inconsistent, or too far gone.

But grace was never about our worthiness; it's about God's character.

Paul, who had once persecuted Christians, became one of the greatest champions of grace. Even as an apostle, he wrestled with weakness and pleaded for God to remove a thorn in his flesh. God's response wasn't healing; it was grace. "My grace is sufficient for you." In other words: "You don't need to be stronger. You need to rely more deeply on Me."

Grace doesn't excuse sin; it empowers us to overcome it. It doesn't ignore weakness, it meets us in it. Grace invites us to come as we are, but it never leaves us there. It transforms us from the inside out, not by pressure but by presence.

To embrace grace means we stop hiding. We stop performing. We stop measuring our worth by our success, discipline, or consistency. Instead, we open our hands, open our hearts, and allow God's love to wash over our shame, soften our striving, and restore our joy.

When you truly grasp grace, your failures no longer define you. Your struggles no longer disqualify you. You begin to live lighter, love deeper, and worship from a place of freedom instead of fear. You extend to others what you've received: kindness, patience, and mercy.

Grace is the heart of the gospel. It's not a one-time pass, it's a daily power. It reminds you that God's strength shines brightest through your surrender.

Application

Take a moment to ask yourself: Where am I still trying to earn what God has already given me? Where am I judging myself more harshly than God does?

Write down one area where you've been self-critical or where shame lingers. Then, beneath it, write this truth: "His grace is sufficient here."

Throughout the day, when you catch yourself spiraling into self-condemnation or pressure to perform, pause. Breathe. And speak aloud: "I am covered by grace. God's power is made perfect in my weakness."

Extend grace to someone else today, especially someone who may not "deserve" it. As you forgive, listen patiently, or show compassion, let it reflect what you've received.

Prayer

Lord, thank You for Your grace, grace that covers my past, meets me in the present, and leads me forward. Help me to stop striving and start receiving. Let Your power be made perfect in my weakness and let my life reflect the beauty of Your mercy. Amen.

Guide Your Thinking:

1. *In what area of my life do I need to stop striving and start receiving grace?*

2. *How does embracing God's grace shift the way I view myself and others?*

_____

_____

_____

_____

_____

_____

_____

_____

DAY 25
Persevering in Prayer

Scripture

"Devote yourselves to prayer, being watchful and thankful."

Colossians 4:2 (NIV)

Reflection

Prayer is not just a spiritual discipline; it's a lifeline. It's the way we connect to the heart of God, hear His voice, express our needs, and align our will with His. But if we're honest, prayer can also feel frustrating. We pray, and sometimes nothing seems to happen. We wait, and answers feel delayed or distant.

This is where perseverance comes in.

Jesus told a story in Luke 18 about a persistent widow who kept asking a judge for justice. She didn't stop, didn't get discouraged, didn't retreat. Eventually, the judge gave in, not because he cared, but because she kept showing up. Jesus used that story to encourage us to "always pray and not give up."

Prayer is not about persuading a reluctant God; it's about partnering with a faithful one. It's not a spiritual vending machine; it's a relational conversation. Sometimes, God answers quickly. Other times, He invites us to keep asking, not to test our patience, but to build our faith and deepen our dependence on Him.

Persevering in prayer means trusting that, even when we don't see the answer, God is still at work. It means believing that every whispered prayer matters, even the ones we barely have the strength to say. It means remembering that the power of prayer lies not in how loudly we speak but in the One who hears us.

Prayer isn't just about getting results; it's about growing relationships. As we stay in conversation with God, our hearts change, even before our circumstances do. We learn to wait with hope, to trust with open hands, and to worship in the in-between.

Sometimes, the greatest breakthroughs are not in what changes around us, but in what changes within us as we persist in prayer. Endurance in prayer doesn't just move mountains, it transforms hearts. It stretches our trust and teaches us to lean not on what we see, but on who He is.

There's power in the prayers you pray when no one's watching. In the tears you cry while interceding. In the groans too deep for words. God hears them all. And in His time, He answers, not always how we expect, but always according to His wisdom and love.

So, don't let silence shake your faith. Don't let delay rob you of intimacy. Keep praying, not because it's easy, but because He is faithful.

Application

Today, identify a prayer you've been tempted to give up on, something you've prayed about for weeks, months, maybe even years. Write it down again. Bring it to God with honesty, not performance.

Commit to praying consistently for that need this week. Set a reminder on your phone or keep a prayer journal. Let persistence become your spiritual posture.

Also, take time to thank God, not just for answered prayers but for the way He's sustaining you while you are waiting. Gratitude fuels perseverance.

Prayer

Lord, teach me to pray with endurance. Help me to trust that You hear me even when the answer hasn't come. Strengthen my faith to keep asking, keep seeking, and keep believing. Draw me closer to You through every conversation. I will not give up, because I know You are faithful. Amen.

Guide Your Thinking:

1. *What have I stopped praying because it feels delayed or impossible?*

2. *How can I build a rhythm of consistent, faith-filled prayer in this season?*

_____

_____

_____

_____

_____

_____

_____

_____

_____

DAY 26
Walking in Freedom

Scripture

"It is for freedom that Christ has set us free. Stand firm, then, and do not let yourselves be burdened again by a yoke of slavery."

Galatians 5:1 (NIV)

Reflection

Freedom is one of the most powerful gifts of the Gospel. But many believers live more like prisoners than like people who've been set free. We carry old shame, rehearse past mistakes, and let fear, addiction, or comparison rule our decisions. We sing about freedom but still live under the weight of what Jesus already broke.

Paul writes in Galatians, "It is for freedom that Christ has set us free." That means freedom isn't just a side benefit; it's the point. Christ didn't die just to forgive you; He died to release you from guilt, from fear, from sin, from the pressure to earn your worth.

To walk in freedom is to accept that you are no longer a slave to your past. You are not defined by what was done to you or what you've done. You are not bound by shame, addiction, or self-hatred. In Christ, you are a new creation. The prison door is open; you just have to walk out.

But here's the challenge: freedom must be maintained. Paul says, "Stand firm, then..." because we're constantly tempted to pick up the chains again. We slide back into old patterns, allow lies to re-enter, or let the opinions of others control our peace. Freedom isn't the absence of struggle; it's the presence of truth. And truth is what sets us free.

Freedom isn't just about what you walk away from; it's also about what you walk toward. You're not just freed from sin; you're freed for purpose. You're free to love without fear, to serve without needing recognition, to rest without guilt, and to worship without shame. This kind of freedom rewires how you live.

And it's not a one-time revelation; it's a daily decision. Freedom must be fought for with intentionality. It means catching toxic thoughts before they spiral, naming lies before they stick, and confronting habits before they harden. It means walking in grace, not just receiving it.

Sometimes the most courageous thing you can do is to believe that you are really free. Free to forgive yourself. Free to try again. Free to not let your past hold your present hostage. That's what Christ paid for, not a half-free life, but a wholly redeemed one.

You don't have to earn freedom; it's already yours. But you do have to walk in it. Every day, with your eyes on Jesus and your heart anchored in truth.

Application

Ask the Holy Spirit to show you any area of your life where you're not living free. Is it a mindset, a relationship, a habit, or a memory that still has control?

Write a declaration based on Scripture (like Romans 8:1 or John 8:36) and speak it aloud: "I am free in Christ, and I will not return to bondage."

Throughout the day, pay attention to moments when guilt, fear, or insecurity try to sneak in. Catch them quickly, and replace them with truth. Walking in freedom means walking in awareness.

Prayer

Jesus, thank You for setting me free. Help me walk in that freedom every day, not bound by my past, but led by Your truth. Show me the places where I've accepted bondage, and teach me to live in the fullness of Your grace. I will not go back. I am free. Amen.

Guide Your Thinking:

1. *What area of my life still feels like a prison, even though Jesus has unlocked the door?*

2. *What lie do I need to replace with truth in order to walk in full freedom?*

_____

_____

_____

_____

_____

_____

_____

_____

_____

DAY 27
Developing a Spirit of Excellence

Scripture

"Whatever you do, work at it with all your heart, as working for the Lord, not for human masters."

Colossians 3:23 (NIV)

Reflection

Excellence is not about perfection; it's about purpose. It's not doing everything flawlessly; it's doing everything faithfully, with your whole heart, as an offering to God. In a culture that often celebrates short-cuts, hustle, and half-hearted effort, a spirit of excellence stands out and glorifies God.

Daniel is a prime example. In a foreign land surrounded by pagan culture, he served with such integrity and excellence that he was promoted again and again. Scripture says he had "an excellent spirit" (Daniel 6:3), and that spirit made room for him in high places, not because he sought position, but because he served with distinction and honor.

Excellence is about more than results; it's about attitude. It's how you show up. It's choosing to be reliable, to do the small things well, to treat others with respect, and to give your best even when no one is watching. Excellence says, "If I'm doing it for God, it's worth doing well."

But excellence can easily become a trap if we confuse it with perfectionism. Perfection strives to impress. Excellence seeks to honor. Perfection is rooted in fear. Excellence flows from love.

Developing a spirit of excellence doesn't mean burning out; it means being intentional. It means caring about the quality of your work, the tone of your voice, the way you serve, and the way you carry your responsibilities, not because you're trying to earn approval, but because you already have God's approval, and now you reflect His nature.

God is excellent in all He does, and as His image-bearers, we're called to reflect that excellence in how we lead, serve, create, and live.

A spirit of excellence is deeply spiritual. It's not about striving for applause, but about cultivating faithfulness in the unseen places. It's showing up on time, preparing diligently, praying over your work, and refusing to cut corners, because you recognize that your life is a reflection of your worship.

Excellence doesn't mean being the best; it means bringing your best. It means stewarding what you've been given and multiplying it with care, intention, and reverence. And it's often in the small, overlooked tasks that this excellence is forged. Washing dishes, sending an email, and responding with kindness are not trivial acts. When done with a heart of worship, they echo into eternity.

Excellence honors God, inspires others, and builds credibility. It makes space for influence that's earned, not demanded. And over time, a life marked by excellence becomes a testimony, not to our greatness, but to God's glory.

Application

Look at one area of your life where you've been coasting, cutting corners, or just going through the motions. Ask God to help you approach that area with renewed passion and purpose.

Whether it's how you work, serve, parent, speak, or lead, commit to doing it as unto the Lord. Ask: Would I do this differently if I were doing it directly for God?

Also, notice your motives. Are you striving to impress people or seeking to honor God? Let His presence, not pressure, fuel your excellence.

Prayer

God, I want to reflect Your excellence in all I do. Help me to serve, speak, and lead with intentionality and love. Teach me to pursue excellence without perfectionism and to give my best not for applause but as worship to You. Amen.

Guide Your Thinking:

1. *In what area of my life have I been settling for "good enough" when God is calling me to greater excellence?*

2. *How can I shift my mindset from performance to purpose?*

_____

_____

_____

_____

_____

_____

_____

_____

DAY 28
Becoming Spiritually Resilient

Scripture

"We are hard pressed on every side, but not crushed; perplexed, but not in despair; persecuted, but not abandoned; struck down, but not destroyed."

2 Corinthians 4:8–9 (NIV)

Reflection

Spiritual resilience is not the denial of pain or the performance of strength. It is the steady decision to remain faithful when circumstances are difficult and outcomes are uncertain. It is the ability to endure hardship without surrendering hope and to continue trusting God when emotions fluctuate. Resilience does not eliminate struggle, but it prevents struggle from defining identity.

Trials reveal what is deeply rooted within us. When pressure intensifies, it exposes whether our confidence rests in comfort or in Christ. If faith depends on favorable conditions, it will weaken when circumstances shift. However, if faith is rooted in God's character, it becomes stronger in the face of adversity. Spiritual resilience grows as we learn to anchor ourselves in truth rather than in temporary stability.

Resilience develops gradually. It is formed through daily obedience, repeated surrender, and continual return to God after disappointment. Each time you choose prayer over panic, trust over fear, and perseverance over retreat, your spiritual endurance increases.

Growth often feels subtle in the moment, but over time, it produces depth and maturity that cannot be manufactured quickly.

James encourages believers to view trials as opportunities for growth, as perseverance leads to spiritual completeness. This perspective does not minimize suffering but recognizes that God uses difficulty to refine faith. When resilience is cultivated, it creates a steadiness that is not shaken easily. It produces confidence that rests not in personal strength but in God's sustaining grace.

Application

Reflect on a current challenge and identify one way it may be strengthening your faith. Write down a specific truth from Scripture that anchors you in this season and return to it daily. Choose one practical act of obedience that reinforces trust in God despite difficulty.

Prayer

God, I'm tired of pretending spiritual strength is always bold and loud. Teach me the holiness of staying. Of long obedience. Of quiet resolve. Make me dura-ble, not by removing the weight, but by making me able to carry it with You. Amen.

Guide Your Thinking:

1. *Where have I been mistaking survival for failure?*

2. *What does it look like to be spiritually durable in my current season, not just inspired?*

_____

_____

END OF WEEK 4
Standing Strong in Storms

You've completed four full weeks of this journey, and this one may have stretched you more than most. This week was about endurance, excellence, freedom, and resilience. It asked more than reflection; it called for resolve. And if you're reading this now, it means you've stayed in the fight, and that matters.

Faith was never meant to be fragile. It's meant to be tested, strengthened, and made steadfast. This week, you've faced the challenge of deep surrender: embracing grace, persevering in prayer, choosing freedom daily, and continuing forward even when the winds of life press hard.

Storms don't just reveal what's inside us, they reveal what's sustaining us. And if this week has taught you anything, it's that God doesn't waste a storm. He uses it to build spiritual muscle, deepen trust, and refine our focus. What may have once shaken you now serves as a place of anchoring.

You're becoming more than a believer; you're becoming a disciple. Someone who doesn't just know the Word but lives it. Someone who doesn't run when it gets hard but leans into grace. Someone who doesn't quit at the first sign of resistance but presses on with a holy kind of grit.

Pause here and take a deep breath. Honor the work God is doing in your life, not just what's changing around you, but what's strengthening within you. You are standing strong, not because life is easy, but because Christ is faithful.

Key Questions to Guide Your Thinking:

1. *What spiritual "storms" have I faced this week, and how did I respond to them?*

2. *Where have I seen evidence of growth in how I handle pressure, pain, or disappointment?*

3. *How have I seen God's strength show up in my weakness?*

4. *Write a prayer thanking God for the endurance He is forming in you, and ask Him to continue equipping you for whatever is ahead.*

_____

_____

_____

_____

_____

_____

_____

_____

_____

_____

_____

_____

_____

_____

_____

_____

_____

Journal

WEEK 5

DAY 29
Restoring Broken Relationships

Scripture

"If it is possible, as far as it depends on you, live at peace with everyone."

Romans 12:18 (NIV)

Reflection

A few things test our character and faith, like fractured relationships. The pain of betrayal, silence, harsh words, or disappointment can leave wounds that seem impossible to heal. And yet, scripture calls us to something higher, something that often feels impossible in our own strength: to pursue peace.

Restoration doesn't mean pretending everything is fine. It doesn't erase the hurt or require you to instantly trust someone who hasn't earned it. What it does require is a heart willing to begin the process, a heart open to healing, reconciliation, or, at the very least, release.

Paul's words in Romans 12:18 carry both grace and challenge: "If it is possible, as far as it depends on you, live at peace with everyone." That means you don't control the outcome, but you do control the posture. You can't force someone to apologize or change, but you can choose forgiveness, humility, and compassion.

And even if full reconciliation never happens, peace can still come. It comes when you release the weight of bitterness, when you pray a blessing over someone who hurt you, when you stop rehearsing the offense and start releasing

it to God. Peace is often less about resolution with others and more about restoration within.

Jesus constantly moved toward the broken. He restored Peter after betrayal, included the tax collector, and made space for the outcast. He never let pride or fear get in the way of love. When we choose to live like Him, we begin to reflect His radical grace, even in the most painful places.

Restoring broken relationships starts with a question: What is mine to own? Where have I contributed to distance or division? Where is God asking me to take a small, humble step, not to control, but to love?

Sometimes, healing begins with a single word: "I'm sorry." Sometimes it's just a prayer: "God, I release them." Other times it's a quiet choice to stay soft, to not retaliate, to trust that God can redeem what feels too far gone.

You may not be able to rebuild the past. But you can invite God to build something new, with peace, humility, and grace as the foundation.

Application

Take time today to reflect on any strained, broken, or painful relationships in your life. Ask the Holy Spirit to bring someone to mind.

Then ask: "What is my role in this? Is there an apology I need to offer? A conversation I need to begin? A burden I need to release?"

Write a prayer for that person, even if reconciliation feels far away. As you do, allow God to soften your heart. Peace often begins in prayer before it's lived out in practice.

Prayer

Lord, you are the God of reconciliation. Show me where I've held onto hurt, pride, or resentment. Give me the courage to take steps toward peace, even when it's hard. Heal what's been broken and let my relationships reflect Your grace and humility. Amen.

Guide Your Thinking:

1. Is there someone I need to forgive, or ask forgiveness from?

2. What would it look like to take one step toward restoring peace in that relationship?

3. How can I surrender the outcome to God while still doing my part?

_____

_____

_____

_____

_____

_____

_____

_____

_____

_____

_____

_____

_____

_____

_____

DAY 30
Gratitude as Resistance in the Wilderness

Scripture

"Though the fig tree does not bud and there are no grapes on the vines... yet I will rejoice in the Lord, I will be joyful in God my Savior."

Habakkuk 3:17–18 (NIV)

Reflection

Gratitude in abundance is natural. Gratitude in lack is supernatural.

The prophet Habakkuk wrote these words not in a moment of celebration but in a season of drought, devastation, and disappointment. Everything around him looked empty. Everything within him could have justified despair. And yet, he chose joy. Not because of what he had but because of who God was.

This is the kind of gratitude that changes atmospheres. It's not naive. It's not performative. It's a bold, Spirit-empowered act of resistance against hopeless-ness. Gratitude in the wilderness becomes a declaration: "Even if I don't see it yet, I will still worship."

There will be seasons in your life that feel barren, where the prayers aren't answered, the breakthrough doesn't come, or the feelings go numb. But even then, you can still give thanks. Not for the pain, but for God's presence in it. Not because it makes sense, but because your spirit remembers He is still good.

Gratitude in these moments trains your soul to focus on what cannot be shaken. It strengthens your trust in the character of God rather than the condition of your circumstances. It reminds your heart that faith is not about what you see, but about who you know.

This kind of gratitude is a spiritual weapon. It keeps your spirit tender. It keeps your mind clear. It shifts the atmosphere of your home, your heart, your relationships. And it roots you in hope, not hype.

If you're in a dry place today, you don't have to fake joy. But you can practice praise. You can whisper thanks for breath in your lungs, for mercy in your mornings, for a God who stays.

Even here. Even now. Especially now.

Application

Take five minutes today to write a gratitude list, not of what's going well, but of what God has remained through. Thank Him for His consistency, His presence, His promises, even if you don't feel them yet.

1. *Then, choose one physical action to embody your gratitude today. That could be:*

2. *Writing a thank-you note to someone who's walked with you in a hard season.*

3. *Go for a short walk and express your thanks to God out loud with each step.*

4. *Post a verse or truth about God's goodness somewhere visible in your space.*

5. *Choosing to end your day not with a scroll but with five minutes of whispered thanks.*

These aren't just exercises; they're acts of spiritual defiance. You are choosing to plant your flag in the soil of faith, even if the landscape feels dry.

Over time, this kind of daily resistance forms holy resilience. It opens your eyes to small miracles. And it trains your heart to see that God's goodness was never dependent on your circumstances, it was always rooted in His unchanging nature.

Prayer

God, I choose to thank You, especially in the wilderness. Teach me to see Your goodness even when life feels heavy. Let my gratitude be more than a response, let it be resistance. A declaration that I trust You, even when I don't understand. Amen.

Guide Your Thinking:

1. *Where have I struggled to give thanks because of disappointment or delay?*

2. *What would it look like to choose gratitude as an act of faith, not just emotion?*

_____

_____

_____

_____

_____

_____

_____

_____

_____

_____

_____

DAY 31
Anchored in Identity

Scripture

"See what great love the Father has lavished on us, that we should be called children of God! And that is what we are!"

1 John 3:1 (NIV)

Reflection

In every season of life, there's one question that echoes beneath the surface of our choices, emotions, and ambitions: Who am I? The world is quick to answer with labels, your job title, your relationship status, your performance, your past. But the only identity that truly holds is the one rooted in the love of God: You are His child.

This truth changes everything.

You are not defined by your worst mistake or your greatest achievement. You're not the sum total of other people's opinions or your own insecurities. You are who God says you are chosen, holy, dearly loved. And yet, how easily we forget.

So often, we live like spiritual orphans, trying to earn love, prove our worth, or hustle for belonging. We perform to be accepted, compare to feel secure and shame ourselves into silence when we fall short. But all the while, God is inviting us to come home, not just to His presence, but to our identity.

Jesus didn't just come to rescue you from sin. He came to restore your identity, to remind you that you belong. That you're not just saved, you're adopted, embraced, and empowered. You don't have to earn your seat at His table. You already have it.

And when you are anchored in that identity, everything changes. You stop chasing affirmation and start walking in confidence. You become less reactive to criticism because your worth isn't up for debate. You love others more freely because you're not competing; you're already secure.

Identity isn't something you build; it's something you receive. It's not based on how you feel today but on what God has declared for eternity.

So the question is not, "Who am I according to my past, my role, or my emotions?"

The real question is, "Who does God say I am, and am I living like it's true?"

Application

Take time today to identify any false identities you've been carrying, labels given by others, shaped by shame or formed through comparison. Write them down. Then, beside each one, write a truth from God's Word that cancels it.

Start your morning tomorrow by declaring, "I am a child of God, fully known, fully loved, fully accepted." Let that truth define your day before the world tries to.

Prayer

Father, thank You for calling me Yours. Remind me daily that I am not what I've done, not what I lack, and not what others say, I am who You say I am. Anchor me in this truth, and let everything I do flow from the confidence of being loved by You. Amen.

Guide Your Thinking:

1. *What have I allowed to define me that God never intended?*

2. *What truth about my identity do I need to not just believe, but begin to live?*

_____

_____

_____

_____

_____

_____

_____

_____

DAY 32
Developing Discernment

Scripture

"The Spirit searches all things, even the deep things of God... The person with the Spirit makes judgments about all things..."

1 Corinthians 2:10,15 (NIV)

Reflection

In a world overflowing with voices, opinions, information, emotion, and noise, discernment is not a luxury; it's a necessity. Without it, we're easily swayed by what sounds right instead of what is right. But discernment isn't just about making good decisions; it's about walking in wisdom guided by the Holy Spirit.

Discernment helps us tune into the frequency of heaven in the middle of earthly confusion. It's the filter that allows us to distinguish between truth and almost-truth, peace and pressure, God's whisper and our own wants. In today's world, discernment guards us not just from deception, but from distraction.

The more we walk closely with Jesus, the more our senses are trained to detect what aligns with His Spirit. That's why discernment is more than instinct, it's intimacy. The closer you are to God, the clearer His voice becomes, and the quicker you are to detect what isn't Him.

But discernment also grows through decisions. Every time you slow down to pray before reacting, seek wisdom rather than rush, or let peace, not pressure, guide your choices, you're practicing spiritual sensitivity. Discernment deepens with each surrendered "yes," each reflective pause, and each moment of obedience.

And discernment isn't just for big moments; it's for daily life. It helps you recognize when a conversation needs grace, when a boundary needs to be set, when a decision should be delayed, or when something that looks good is actually not God's best.

Jesus didn't make choices based on convenience or crowd approval. He moved with intentionality, always in sync with the Father. And that's our model. When we grow in discernment, we stop living reactive lives and start living responsive ones, guided not by trends but by truth.

In a culture of chaos, discernment is your anchor. In a world full of noise, it's your compass. And in your daily walk, it's a gift you can ask for, grow in, and rely on.

Application

Ask the Holy Spirit today for the gift of discernment. Write down a decision or situation you're facing that requires wisdom. Pause before rushing into action, pray, reflect, and ask: "What is God really saying here?"

Spend time in God's Word, specifically Proverbs or the Gospels, and ask Him to train your spiritual instincts. Over time, discernment grows stronger through daily surrender, not instant downloads.

Also, invite wise counsel into your life. Discernment is sharpened in commu-nity, not isolation.

Prayer

Holy Spirit, I need Your discernment. Quiet the noise around me so I can hear Your voice clearly. Teach me to see beneath the surface, to respond to Your promptings, and to walk in wisdom. Let my decisions reflect Your truth and not just my instincts. Amen.

Guide Your Thinking:

1. *Where in my life do I need greater discernment right now?*

2. *What would change if I slowed down to listen before I moved?*

_____

_____

_____

_____

_____

_____

_____

_____

DAY 33
Walking in Spiritual Authority

Scripture

"I have given you authority... to overcome all the power of the enemy; nothing will harm you."

Luke 10:19 (NIV)

Reflection

Many believers live far below their spiritual inheritance, not because they lack power, but because they don't understand their authority. We often pray from a place of pleading when Jesus has called us to stand from a place of victory.

Spiritual authority isn't about position, it's about identity. When you know who you are in Christ, you begin to walk differently. You pray with boldness, resist the enemy with confidence, and step into difficult situations knowing you are not alone; you are commissioned.

Jesus gave His followers authority to drive out demons, heal the sick, and proclaim the Kingdom. That wasn't just for the apostles; it's for you. Not because you're strong but because He is. Not because you've earned it but because you've been entrusted with it.

The enemy's greatest tactic is to convince you that you're powerless. That you have to live in fear, shame, or defeat. But Jesus has already won the war; you're not fighting for victory; you're fighting from it. And the authority He gives isn't limited to church moments, it's for your family, your workplace, your thought life, and your spiritual battles.

When you walk in spiritual authority, you stop tolerating what Jesus died to break. You start aligning your words, choices, and prayers with heaven's truth, not earth's chaos.

But authority requires alignment. It's not about doing whatever you want in God's name; it's about being so submitted to His will that His power flows through your life. Humility isn't weakness; it's the posture of those trusted with authority.

So lift your head today. Speak truth over your life. Push back the darkness with praise. Intercede boldly for your family. Reject fear. Bind lies. Declare freedom. You are a child of the King, and you carry His authority.

Application

Ask yourself: Have I been living like someone who has authority in Christ, or like someone just trying to survive?

Choose one area of your life where fear or chaos has tried to take hold. Find a scripture that speaks truth over that area (e.g., 2 Timothy 1:7, James 4:7, Ephesians 6:10–18), and begin declaring it daily.

Speak with boldness today. Pray not as a beggar, but as a son or daughter of the King.

Prayer

Jesus, thank You for the authority You've entrusted to me. Teach me to walk in it, not with pride, but with power. Help me recognize the spiritual battles I'm facing and respond with truth, not fear. Let my life reflect the victory You've already won. Amen.

Guide Your Thinking:

1. *In what area of my life have I been forgetting the authority I carry in Christ?*

2. *What would change if I lived like I truly believed victory was already mine?*

_____

_____

_____

_____

_____

_____

_____

_____

DAY 34
Pursuing God's Presence Daily

Scripture

"You will seek me and find me when you seek me with all your heart."

Jeremiah 29:13 (NIV)

Reflection

God's presence is not just a concept to study; it's a reality to live in. It's not reserved for Sunday mornings or worship nights; it's available in the ordinary, sacred moments of your everyday life. The question isn't "Is God here?" The question is, "Am I aware of Him?"

We often treat God's presence like a destination we visit, rather than a dwelling place we live in. But from the beginning, God's desire was not just to be acknowledged, it was to be with us. To walk with us in the cool of the day. To inhabit not just the temple but our hearts.

Moses understood this. When offered blessings, victory, and a promised land, he still said, "If your Presence does not go with us, do not send us up from here." (Exodus 33:15). He valued God's presence more than progress. More than success. More than the promise itself.

The presence of God quiets fear, clarifies confusion, and fills emptiness. It's where burdens are lifted, and hearts are softened. But it doesn't happen by acci-dent. It happens through pursuit.

To pursue God's presence daily is to build your life around Him, not just include Him. It's pausing in the middle of a busy day to worship. It's turning off the noise to listen. It's choosing Scripture before scrolling, prayer before panic, and stillness before striving.

His presence doesn't demand perfection, it invites honesty. You don't have to clean yourself up to draw near. You just have to come. He meets the hungry. He fills the thirsty. He draws near to those who draw near to Him.

And the more time you spend with Him, the more you become like Him. That's the gift of His presence; it doesn't just comfort you; it transforms you.

Application

Set aside intentional time today to pursue God, not with an agenda, but with hunger. Turn on worship music, find a quiet place, or take a walk and pray aloud. Simply say, "God, I want to be with You."

Create a daily rhythm this week to make space for His presence, five minutes of stillness, scripture meditation, or silent worship before anything else.

Ask yourself daily: "Am I living aware of God's nearness right now?"

Prayer

God, I don't want to visit Your presence; I want to dwell in it. Teach me to seek You daily, not out of duty, but out of desire. Let Your nearness be my peace, my direction, and my joy. Stir in me a deeper hunger to know You, not just what You can do, but who You are. Amen.

Guide Your Thinking:

1. *What has been distracting me from daily intimacy with God?*

2. *What simple shift can I make this week to prioritize His presence over everything else?*

_____

_____

_____

_____

_____

_____

_____

_____

_____

DAY 35
Staying Rooted in Community

Scripture

"And let us consider how we may spur one another on toward love and good deeds, not giving up meeting together... but encouraging one another."

Hebrews 10:24–25 (NIV)

Reflection

God never intended for you to walk this journey of faith alone. From Genesis to Revelation, scripture reveals a consistent truth: transformation happens in togetherness. Healing, strength, accountability, and growth flourish in the soil of a spiritual community.

And yet, many believers live disconnected, isolated by busyness, past wounds, pride, or fear. We say things like, "I'll figure it out myself," or "I don't need anyone," while slowly drifting into spiritual dryness. But isolation is dangerous, not just emotionally, but spiritually. The enemy loves nothing more than a lone believer because we're most vulnerable when we're unguarded and alone.

The early Church understood the power of community. They broke bread together, prayed together, carried each other's burdens, and met needs with radical generosity. Their unity wasn't built on convenience; it was built on commitment.

Real community is messy. It requires vulnerability, forgiveness, patience, and grace. It means showing up when it's uncomfortable and leaning in when it's easier to withdraw. But it's also the place where iron sharpens iron, where encouragement flows, and where spiritual gifts collide to build something stronger than any one of us could build alone.

To stay rooted in community is to prioritize relationships that nourish your soul and challenge your spirit. It's saying, "I won't just attend, I will belong. I won't just consume, I will contribute." Because the Church isn't a service, it's a family. And you are needed.

Whether you're in a small group, serving team, prayer circle, or a trusted circle of believers, plant yourself. Root deep. Show up. Be known. The strength of your spiritual life is often tied to the strength of your spiritual relationships.

Application

Reflect on your current level of spiritual community. Are you deeply connected, or drifting? Who knows your story, your struggles, your gifts?

Reach out to one person this week and be honest. If you're not in a small group or accountability circle, pray about taking that step. If you are, ask how you can go deeper, not just showing up but investing fully.

And if you've been hurt by the community in the past, ask God to heal and guide you toward the right relationships today.

Prayer

Lord, thank You for the gift of community. Forgive me for the ways I've with-drawn or tried to walk alone. Help me to plant myself in relationships that honor You and sharpen me. Teach me to give and receive, to support and be supported. Let my life reflect Your love in how I live with others. Amen.

Guide Your Thinking:

1. *Am I deeply rooted in a spiritual community, or am I spiritually isolated?*

2. *What step can I take this week to grow deeper in connection, accountability, and love?*

_____

_____

_____

_____

_____

_____

_____

_____

_____

END OF WEEK 5
Living from a Renewed Mindset

This week was about more than new habits, it was about new thinking. Each day invited you to see differently, speak differently, and live with a renewed awareness of who God is, who you are in Him, and how that truth transforms everything.

From anchoring your identity in Christ to developing spiritual discernment, walking in authority, pursuing God's presence, and staying rooted in community, you've been practicing the mind of Christ. That's not small. That's sacred.

Romans 12:2 says we are transformed by the renewing of our minds. That renewal happens when you stop living by reaction and start living by revelation. When you no longer let culture, fear, or past pain define you, but instead let God's Word reshape you from the inside out.

This kind of mindset shift doesn't happen in a moment, it's a lifelong process. But each reflection, each prayer, each small step of obedience is chiseling away old thinking and carving space for truth. You're not just adjusting your thoughts, you're becoming someone new.

Think about this past week: What lie was exposed? What old pattern lost its grip? What truth stuck with you and started changing how you show up in life?

Let that progress fuel your next step. You're halfway through this journey, and God has already done much. But He's not finished.

As your mindset continues to shift, your capacity for joy, purpose, freedom, and spiritual authority will only grow.

Don't rush past this moment. Reflect. Celebrate. And get ready, because what God has started in your mind is about to move into every part of your life.

Key Questions to Guide Your Thinking:

1. *How has my mindset changed in the past week?*

2. *What thought patterns or beliefs has God been inviting me to surrender or replace?*

3. *What daily practice has helped me stay renewed, and how can I keep that rhythm going?*

4. *Write a prayer of gratitude for the mental and spiritual shifts that have taken place, and ask God to continue renewing your heart and mind.*

_____

_____

_____

_____

_____

_____

_____

_____

_____

_____

_____

_____

Journal

_____
_____
_____
_____
_____
_____
_____
_____
_____
_____
_____
_____
_____
_____
_____
_____
_____
_____
_____
_____
_____
_____
_____
_____
_____
_____

WEEK 6

DAY 36
Living with Eternal Perspective

Scripture

"So we fix our eyes not on what is seen, but on what is unseen, since what is seen is temporary, but what is unseen is eternal."

2 Corinthians 4:18 (NIV)

Reflection

Most of us live with our eyes on the immediate, today's demands, this week's schedule, and next month's goals. And while God cares deeply about the details of our lives, He also invites us to zoom out, to live not just for the moment but for eternity.

An eternal perspective doesn't detach you from reality; it redefines it. It lifts your eyes from temporary troubles and fixes them on the lasting truth. It's the ability to live grounded in heaven's priorities while navigating earth's responsibilities.

Paul understood this. He endured shipwrecks, beatings, imprisonment, and rejection, but he didn't give up. Why? Because his eyes weren't fixed on comfort, they were fixed on the Kingdom. He saw his life through the lens of eternity. Every trial became a light; momentary affliction compared to the glory ahead.

When you live with an eternal perspective, you start asking different questions. Not just "What feels good right now?" but "What matters forever?" Not just, "How can I win?" but "How can I serve?" Not just, "What do I want?" but, "What is God building through me that will outlast me?"

It's so easy to get caught up in what's urgent and miss what's ultimate. But the more we align with God's eternal purposes, the more peace and purpose we experience in the present. Living for eternity doesn't mean you ignore the here and now; it means you live in the here and now with the weight of forever in your heart.

Your job may be temporary, but your faithfulness there has an eternal impact. Your unseen prayers? Eternal. The quiet sacrifices no one applauds. Eternal. The love you extend when it costs you something. Eternal.

Living with eternity in mind gives you staying power. It helps you forgive faster, love deeper, and serve longer. It reminds you that discomfort doesn't mean defeat, and delay doesn't mean denial. Eternity reframes your perspective, turning today's setbacks into setups for something greater.

So when the road feels long and the rewards invisible, remind yourself: this isn't the finish line. You're building something that can't be burned, broken, or erased. Something heaven celebrates even when earth overlooks.

This life is a mist, a breath, a blink. But what we build in Christ lasts forever.

Application

Spend a few moments today evaluating your focus. Where have your thoughts, time, and energy been invested lately? Are they fueling only the temporary, or are they building what will last?

Make a list of what has eternal value in your current season: relationships, spiritual growth, serving others, and discipleship. Ask God to help you invest more deeply in those things.

Prayer

Lord, teach me to number my days and live for what truly matters. Help me fix my eyes on what is unseen, not because I want to escape this world, but because I want to live in it with eternity in mind. Shift my priorities. Realign my heart. And let my life be a reflection of forever. Amen.

Guide Your Thinking:

1. *What would shift in my daily decisions if I lived with eternity in view?*

2. *Where do I need to exchange short-term comfort for long-term purpose?*

_____

_____

_____

_____

_____

_____

_____

_____

DAY 37
Standing in Spiritual Confidence

Scripture

*"So do not throw away your confidence;
it will be richly rewarded."*

Hebrews 10:35 (NIV)

Reflection

Confidence is often misunderstood. The world says confidence is found in self, in what you can do, how you perform, and what others think of you. But spiritual confidence isn't rooted in self-assurance; it's rooted in God-assurance. It's the deep, quiet strength that comes from knowing who you belong to, what He has spoken, and where your help comes from.

We all face moments that shake us, delays, disappointments, or spiritual battles that leave us wondering if we have what it takes. But Hebrews reminds us not to throw away our confidence because it holds rich reward. Confidence, in God's eyes, is not arrogance; it's faith in action. It's standing when everything in you wants to run. It's trusting when answers haven't come. It's declaring truth even when fear is screaming.

Confidence doesn't come from your performance. It comes from your position, seated with Christ, covered by grace, filled with the Spirit. When you understand that, you don't walk timidly; you walk boldly. Not because you're invincible, but because He is with you.

Remember David? He didn't face Goliath with false bravado. He stood before a giant with holy confidence, not in his slingshot, but in the God who had never failed him. That same God fights for you.

So many of us hide when we should be standing. We second-guess when we should be speaking. We shrink back when we're called to rise up. But God is calling you into a confidence that's not loud, but unwavering. Not self-made, but Spirit-led.

You were not created to be paralyzed by fear or silenced by insecurity. You were made to stand, to stand in truth, in grace, and in authority. When you walk in that confidence, you reflect the heart of a God who does not waver.

Application

Where have you been playing small because of fear or self-doubt? Write it down.

Then, ask God to show you a scripture to anchor your confidence. Meditate on it, declare it aloud, and speak it over that very place of insecurity.

Take one bold step today, whether it's sharing your story, starting that conversation, or simply showing up with courage. Let your confidence come not from your ability, but from His presence.

Prayer

Father, I've doubted myself more than I've trusted You. But today, I reclaim my confidence, not in my strength, but in Yours. Remind me that I am chosen, equipped, and covered. Help me to stand with boldness, speak with truth, and walk in the fullness of who You've called me to be. Amen.

Guide Your Thinking:

1. *What has caused me to shrink back when God is calling me to stand?*

2. *What truth about who I am in Christ do I need to declare more boldly?*

_____

_____

_____

_____

_____

_____

_____

_____

_____

_____

_____

_____

_____

_____

_____

_____

_____

_____

_____

DAY 38
Guarding the Heart in a Distracted World

Scripture

"Above all else, guard your heart,
for everything you do flows from it."

Proverbs 4:23 (NIV)

Reflection

Your heart is a sacred space, the wellspring of your desires, your thoughts, your convictions, and your worship. And yet, we often treat it carelessly, allowing unfiltered voices, distractions, and emotional clutter to take root without even realizing it.

The writer of Proverbs offers a strong and urgent command: "Above all else, guard your heart." Not your reputation. Not your schedule. Not even your comfort. But your heart. Why? Because everything else flows from there, your choices, your responses, your relationships, your sense of identity and purpose.

The world is loud. Our culture thrives on reaction, stimulation, and comparison. Every scroll, notification, headline, or heated conversation has the potential to shape what we believe, how we feel, and ultimately, how we live. If we're not careful, our hearts become open gates, absorbing everything, good, bad, and toxic.

Guarding your heart isn't about fear or control; it's about discernment. It means living with spiritual awareness, recognizing that not everything that is allowed access should be. It means filtering what you consume, being honest about what's influencing you, and learning to walk away from things that seem harmless but chip away at your spiritual health over time.

Jesus modeled this beautifully. He didn't allow the noise of the crowd or the agenda of others to rule His heart. He slipped away often to be alone with the Father. He chose solitude over applause, prayer over pressure, and truth over popularity. That's how He stayed centered, anchored in love, truth, and divine clarity.

Guarding your heart also means being honest about what's already inside. What bitterness have you let grow unchecked? What insecurities are shaping your decisions? What hidden idols or distractions have found a home in your soul?

This isn't about shame, it's about freedom. When you intentionally guard your heart, you begin to notice subtle shifts. You become more peaceful, more rooted, less reactive. Your appetite for noise lessens. Your hunger for God grows.

Your heart is the home of your intimacy with God. Guard it like it's worth everything, because it is.

Application

Take 15 quiet minutes today. No music. No phone. Just silence. Ask the Holy Spirit: "What have I let into my heart that needs to go?"

Write down anything that comes up, voices, thoughts, habits, distractions. Then ask: "What do you want to replace it with?" Listen for His invitation.

Prayer

Father, I've let too much into my heart without asking if it belongs. I've allowed distractions to dull my hunger and outside voices to shape my worth. Today, I want to guard my heart, not out of fear, but in wisdom. Show me what needs to go and what needs to grow. Make my heart a place where Your presence dwells freely. Amen.

Guide Your Thinking:

1. *What have I been consuming (mentally, emotionally, spiritually) that is shaping my heart in unhelpful ways?*

2. *What new habits can I build to guard my heart and deepen my awareness of God's purpose?*

_____

_____

_____

_____

_____

_____

_____

_____

_____

DAY 39
Becoming Spiritually Disciplined Without Legalism

Scripture

"Train yourself to be godly. For physical training is of some value, but godliness has value for all things…"

1 Timothy 4:7–8 (NIV)

Reflection

Discipline. For many, the word carries weight, maybe even baggage. It brings to mind rigid routines, religious checklists, or the exhausting pressure to "do more" for God. But true spiritual discipline isn't about earning approval. It's about aligning your life with the One you already belong to.

Paul told Timothy to "train yourself to be godly," comparing spiritual growth to physical training. Why? Because just as the body requires exercise, the soul requires rhythm: intentional, consistent practices that make room for transformation. But the goal isn't behavior modification, it's heart formation.

This is where legalism often creeps in. Legalism says, "Do this, or God won't love you." Discipline says, "Do this because God already loves you, and you want to be close to Him." The difference is everything.

Discipline without love leads to striving. Love without discipline often leads to stagnation. But when you combine grace and grit, anchoring your routines in relationship, you step into a life that's both grounded and growing.

Jesus had discipline. He withdrew to pray, studied scripture, fasted, and lived with intention. But He wasn't checking boxes; He was communing with the Father. His discipline flowed from desire.

What if your disciplines, prayer, reading, rest, fasting, serving, became less about obligation and more about creating space for God to speak, shape, and renew you? What if you stopped counting missed days and started focusing on meeting with Him?

Spiritual discipline is not the enemy of grace; it's the expression of it. It's saying, "God, I want to grow with You, and I'm willing to show up even when I don't feel it."

You won't always feel motivated. But that's not failure, it's formation. Discipline teaches you to show up not because you feel close to God but because you want to be. And over time, those small moments of faithfulness become the groundwork for spiritual maturity.

Don't confuse discipline with distance. If God feels far, He hasn't moved. Maybe He's waiting for you in the quiet place, no pressure, no shame. Just an open invitation to come and grow.

Application

Reflect on your current spiritual habits. Which ones are life-giving? Which ones feel performative or heavy?

Ask God to reframe your approach. Choose one spiritual discipline to engage this week, not as a task, but as an invitation. Approach it with grace and curiosity, not guilt.

Prayer

God, help me to see spiritual discipline not as pressure but as an opportunity to meet with You. Strip away performance, pride, and shame. Plant in me a hunger for consistency rooted in love. Train me to be godly, not so I can prove myself, but so I can be more like You. Amen.

Guide Your Thinking:

1. *Have I confused spiritual discipline with spiritual performance?*

2. *What's one practice I can approach this week with fresh perspective and joy?*

_____
_____
_____
_____
_____
_____
_____
_____

DAY 40
Serving from Overflow, Not Emptiness

Scripture

"Whoever believes in me, as scripture has said, rivers of living water will flow from within them."

John 7:38 (NIV)

Reflection

Serving is beautiful. It's Christlike. It's powerful. But serving without rest, without connection, without presence, quickly turns into burnout. And burnout doesn't glorify God. It drains you, frustrates others, and often leads to silent bitterness beneath your once joyful "yes."

Jesus calls us to serve from a place of overflow, not exhaustion.
From living waters, not dry wells.

But here's the tension: it's entirely possible to do all the right things for God, without actually doing them with God. To be busy for Him and yet distant from Him. You can lead the team, preach the message, raise the kids, support your friends, and still be running on spiritual fumes.

Jesus never intended you to be the source, He intended you to stay connected to the Source. He said, "Remain in me, and you will bear much fruit." Not strive harder. Not produce under pressure. Remain.

Overflow doesn't come from trying harder. It comes from slowing down. It comes from real connection rooted in prayer, presence, and intimacy. When you're full of God's love, His truth, His joy, it naturally spills out into your service. You serve not to earn but to extend what you've already received.

And sometimes, the holiest thing you can do is step back, not to quit, but to refill. Jesus withdrew often. Not because He was weak, but because He was wise. If the Son of God needed time alone with the Father to sustain His ministry, so do you.

If serving has become heavy, if joy has been replaced with duty, if your "yes" is more from guilt than grace, it's time to pause. Not to walk away from what God's called you to, but to remember why He called you in the first place: not just to serve Him, but to be with Him.

Application

Check your spiritual tank today. Are you serving from overflow or from depletion?

Take time to be still in God's presence, not to prepare, lead, or teach. Just to receive. Let Him fill the places where you've been running dry.

If needed, take a Sabbath from serving this week. Ask for help. Let God remind you that your value is not in what you do but in who you are to Him.

Prayer

Jesus, I confess that I've sometimes served others while neglecting my own soul. Fill me again, not with tasks, but with Your presence. Let every act of service come from a full heart, not an empty one. Teach me to remain in You, to rest in You, and to pour out only what You've poured in. Amen.

Guide Your Thinking:

1. *Am I currently serving from overflow, or from emptiness?*

2. *What do I need to say no to this week so I can say yes to being filled again?*

DAY 41
Letting God Reframe Your Story

Scripture

"And we know that in all things God works for the good of those who love him, who have been called according to his purpose."

Romans 8:28 (NIV)

Reflection

Everyone has a story. And most stories have moments we wish we could erase, wounds, regrets, mistakes, or seasons we didn't choose. We carry these chapters quietly, sometimes believing they disqualify us from being fully used by God.

But here's the truth: God doesn't discard broken stories; He rewrites them.

Romans 8:28 isn't a cliché; it's a promise. God doesn't just redeem the good parts. He works in all things. That means even the dark pages, the failures, the years that feel wasted, the places you thought would break you, those too can be woven into something beautiful.

Reframing your story isn't about pretending it didn't hurt. It's about allowing God to redefine what that chapter means. It's choosing to say, "This didn't destroy me, it deepened me. This didn't define me, it developed me." Through His eyes, what once looked like ruin begins to look like redemption.

Consider Joseph. Betrayed by his brothers, thrown in a pit, forgotten in prison, his story could've ended bitterly. But God reframed it. And in Genesis 50:20, Joseph told his brothers, "You intended to harm me, but God intended it for good..." That's the power of divine perspective.

Your story might not be tidy. It might still be unfolding. But it's not over. And with God, no part is wasted. The detours, delays, and disappointments can all become places of healing for others. Your scars become signposts of His grace.

Letting God reframe your story is an act of faith. It's giving Him the pen and trusting that even if you wouldn't have written it this way, He is still the Author, and He is still good.

Application

Reflect on a part of your story you've struggled to accept or share. Write it down without editing, just honesty.

Now ask God: "How do You see this part of my story?" Sit with that question in prayer. Ask for healing, reframing, and the courage to trust Him with even the unfinished parts.

Prayer

Father, there are parts of my story that still ache. But I believe You are a Redeemer. Help me surrender the broken places to You. Reframe what I can't fix. Heal what I can't explain. And let my life be a testimony of Your goodness, even in the places I once wanted to hide. Amen.

Guide Your Thinking:

1. *What chapter of my story have I tried to forget, instead of giving to God for redemption?*

2. *How might my past become a place of healing and ministry for others?*

_____

_____

_____

_____

_____

_____

_____

_____

DAY 42
Living Unoffended in a Critical Culture

Scripture

"A person's wisdom yields patience; it is to one's glory to overlook an offense."

Proverbs 19:11 (NIV)

Reflection

We live in a culture that's quick to be offended and slow to forgive. Offense is everywhere, online, in families, friendships, churches, and even in the mirror. And while offense may be common, staying offended is not your calling. As a citizen of the Kingdom, you are called to a higher way.

Proverbs 19:11 says it is to one's glory to overlook an offense. That doesn't mean ignoring abuse or enabling injustice. It means choosing not to carry petty insults, harsh words, misunderstandings, or criticism like bricks in your soul. It means choosing peace over pettiness and unity over ego.

Jesus lived unoffended. He was misunderstood, falsely accused, betrayed, and abandoned. Yet He never allowed bitterness to take root. From the cross, He didn't retaliate; He interceded. "Father, forgive them…" Those words didn't come from passivity; they came from power. The power of love.

When you live unoffended, you don't pretend things don't hurt. You just refuse to let those wounds harden your heart. You set boundaries, speak truth, and walk in grace. You choose forgiveness, not because the offense was okay, but because freedom is better than bitterness.

Offense thrives in pride. It feeds on self-righteousness and demands repayment. But the Spirit of God invites us to let go, not to become doormats, but to become free. The longer you hold an offense, the deeper its roots grow, and the harder it becomes to love the way Christ loves.

What if we stopped being easily offended and started being deeply secure in who we are in Christ? What if we refused to mirror the outrage of the world and instead modeled the compassion of the King?

Choosing to live unoffended may feel costly but carrying offense costs more. It steals joy, poisons relationships, and clouds your view of God and others.

Lay it down. Again and again, if you must. This is Kingdom living.

Application

Ask the Holy Spirit to reveal if you're carrying offenses toward a person, group, leader, or even yourself.

Write down their name (or situation). Then, pray intentionally: "Lord, I choose forgiveness. Help me release what I cannot fix. Heal what I cannot explain."

If safe and appropriate, consider reaching out in reconciliation, or simply choose to bless them in prayer.

Prayer

Jesus, teach me to live unoffended. Heal the places where bitterness has taken root. Help me choose grace over resentment, love over judgment, and peace over pride. Let my life reflect the freedom of one who has been deeply forgiven. Amen.

Guide Your Thinking:

1. *Who or what do I need to release today to walk in freedom?*

2. *How can I respond more like Jesus when I feel misunderstood or hurt?*

END OF WEEK 6
Living with Eternal Perspective

You've now completed six weeks on this journey, forty-two days of showing up, seeking God, and saying yes to becoming. This week has likely stirred some deep things in your soul. You've confronted areas of control, exhaustion, offense, distraction, and spiritual drift. But more than that, you've begun to see your life, and your story, through a different lens: eternity.

Living with eternal perspective isn't about escaping the present. It's about being grounded in what truly lasts while walking through what's temporary. It's choosing substance over surface. Character over comfort. Legacy over applause. And this week, you've practiced doing just that.

You surrendered control and allowed God to reframe your story. You were reminded that discipline flows from love, not performance. You took time to check the condition of your heart, to rest when needed, to let go of offenses, and to remember that every moment, every "yes", carries eternal weight.

God is not only writing your story, but He's also anchoring you in His. And nothing is wasted. Not your tears. Not your questions. Not you're waiting. He's forming something deeper in you that will outlast circumstances and extend beyond this life.

Take a moment to honor the work God has done this week. Reflect on how your thinking has shifted. Revisit the Scriptures and truths that sparked something new in you. These aren't just good devotionals; they are deposits of Kingdom truth meant to rewire the way you live.

Let eternity keep shaping your priorities. Let the peace of God guard your heart. And let your life continue to reflect not what is urgent, but what is ultimate.

You are becoming someone who lives with heaven in view.

Key Questions to Guide Your Thinking:

1.   *What truth this week has shifted my focus the most?*

2.   *Where am I still tempted to live for the approval of man instead of the applause of heaven?*

3.   *What practical rhythms can help me keep eternity at the center of my daily decisions?*

_____

_____

_____

_____

_____

_____

_____

_____

_____

Journal

WEEK 7

DAY 43
Developing Consistency in Character

Scripture

"Whoever can be trusted with very little can also be trusted with much..."

Luke 16:10 (NIV)

Reflection

Your character is who you are when no one's watching. It's not your reputation, it's your reality. And in the Kingdom of God, consistency of character matters more than charisma, more than gifting, even more than influence.

We live in a culture obsessed with quick success and visible platforms. But God is interested in the foundation. The quiet, hidden places where integrity is built, trust is forged, and your private world aligns with your public life.

Jesus said, "If you can be trusted with little, you can be trusted with much." That means how you handle the "small" things, your words, your time, your habits, your treatment of people who can't benefit you, matters deeply. These unseen moments reveal who you're becoming.

Consistency in character doesn't mean perfection. It means alignment. It's not about never messing up; it's about being honest when you do. It's about making daily choices that match the values you claim to live by. When you're rooted in Christ, your character becomes stable, even when circumstances aren't.

Consider Daniel. Even when threatened with death, he continued praying as he always had. His consistency in the quiet gave him strength in the storm. He didn't need to panic in a crisis because he had already been faithful in secret.

The truth is that your calling will take you only as far as your character can sustain you. Gifting may open doors, but character keeps them open. And the fruit of the Spirit, love, patience, self-control, kindness, can't be faked for long. They are grown in daily, Spirit-led surrender.

Who you're becoming matters more than what you're producing. God isn't impressed by your hustle; He's moved by your heart.

But here's the grace: consistency is built one decision at a time. It's choosing faithfulness when no one applauds. It's honoring your word, even when it costs you. It's responding with integrity, even when others don't. These moments might seem small, but in God's economy, they are weighty. They are the building blocks of legacy.

And when you fail (because we all do), don't be discouraged. Return to the root. Repent, realign, and keep growing. God isn't looking for perfection; He's looking for perseverance.

Let your life preach louder than your lips. Let your consistency be your greatest testimony, not because you never fell, but because you kept rising, kept showing up, kept choosing Christ in the everyday decisions that no one but heaven sees.

Application

Reflect today on the private areas of your life, your thought life, speech, time management, and how you treat others in hidden spaces.

Ask: "Where is there a gap between what I believe and how I behave?"

Choose one small area where you can begin showing up more consistently, with integrity, discipline, or grace. Let the Holy Spirit guide your steps.

Prayer

Father, I want my life to reflect You, not just in public, but in private. Shape my character. Align my heart with my actions. Help me become consistent in the small things so that I can be trusted with more. Let my life be marked by integrity, humility, and steady faith. Amen.

Guide Your Thinking:

1. *Where is God inviting me to become more consistent in my character?*

2. *What habits or compromises might be weakening my foundation?*

_____

_____

_____

_____

_____

_____

_____

_____

DAY 44
Spiritual Curiosity, Asking God Better Questions

Scripture

"Call to me and I will answer you and tell you great and unsearchable things you do not know."

Jeremiah 33:3 (NIV)

Reflection

Somewhere along the line, many of us were taught that faith means certainty. That mature Christians don't wrestle, don't wonder, don't ask too many questions. But scripture tells a different story, one filled with seekers, strugglers, and saints who brought their deepest questions to God.

Abraham asked, "Will You sweep away the righteous with the wicked?"

David cried out, "How long, Lord?"

Mary wondered, "How can this be?"

Jesus, in agony, asked, "My God, why have You forsaken me?"

These weren't signs of doubt; they were expressions of a raw, real relationship. God isn't threatened by your curiosity. He invites it. Not to test your faith but to deepen it.

Spiritual curiosity is different from skepticism. Skepticism demands answers on its own terms. Curiosity comes with humility. It says, "I want to know You more, even if I don't fully understand You." It creates space for mystery, trust, and awe. And in that space, your faith becomes personal, not just something inherited or memorized but wrestled with and owned.

Jesus often responded to questions with more questions, not to confuse, but to invite people into deeper reflection. He knew the power of curiosity to soften hearts and spark transformation. The most life-changing revelations often begin not with declarations but with a question whispered in prayer: "God, what are You trying to show me here?"

Asking better questions shifts your spiritual posture. Instead of just praying, "God, fix this," you begin to pray, "God, what are You forming in me through this?" Instead of asking, "Why is this happening?" you begin asking, "How can I walk with You through it?"

When you embrace curiosity, your relationship with God becomes more alive, more honest, and more transformative. You move from performance to pursuit. From routine to revelation. You realize that questions aren't detours from faith; they're often the doorway to deeper intimacy.

What question is God waiting for you to ask?

Application

Carve out time today for a quiet moment with God. In your journal or prayer time, write three honest, heart-level questions you've been afraid to ask Him. Sit with them in prayer. Don't rush for answers, listen for His presence in the waiting.

Prayer

Father, thank You for being a God who invites questions. I don't want a surface-level relationship with you, I want depth, honesty, and intimacy. Teach me to be brave in my curiosity. Let my questions lead me not into doubt but into deeper dependence. In You, may I find both mystery and meaning. Amen.

Guide Your Thinking:

1. *What's one question I've been too afraid or too busy to ask God?*

2. *How would my faith grow if I stopped avoiding the questions and started exploring them with Him?*

_____

_____

_____

_____

_____

_____

_____

_____

_____

DAY 45
Pacing with God, Learning the Rhythm of Grace

Scripture

"Come to me, all you who are weary and burdened, and I will give you rest... Learn from me... For my yoke is easy and my burden is light."

Matthew 11:28–30 (NIV)

Reflection

We live in a world that glorifies speed. Faster is better. Hustle is honored. Rest is often mistaken for weakness. And without even realizing it, we begin living at a pace that outruns our peace.

But God doesn't rush transformation. He is not in a hurry with your story. He moves with intentional, unforced rhythms. And if we want to walk closely with Him, we must learn to move at His pace, not the world's.

Jesus never hurried. He was always present, always aware of the moment, always in tune with the Father's timing. Whether He was healing one person or feeding five thousand, He carried a rhythm of grace. And He invites you into that same rhythm, not one of performance or burnout, but of rest and purpose.

In Matthew 11, Jesus doesn't just offer rest from physical exhaustion. He offers rest for your soul. That kind of rest comes not from doing less, but from walking differently. He says, "Take my yoke upon you and learn from me." A yoke joins two oxen so they can move together in sync. That's the image Jesus uses to invite you into a pace, not a sprint, not a struggle, but a shared journey.

When you run ahead of God, you burn out. When you lag behind, you become anxious. But when you walk with Him, you find a pace that feels like peace.

Pacing with God doesn't mean your life will be slow, it means it will be sustainable. It means you'll know when to rest when to move when to say yes, and when to say no. It means you stop measuring your worth by productivity and start measuring it by proximity, how close am I to Jesus right now?

This pace requires trust. Trust that God's timing is perfect. Trust that delays are not denials. Trust that even when it feels like you're not doing enough, God is still doing something in you.

Slow down today, not just physically, but spiritually. Ask, "Am I walking with God, or trying to get ahead of Him?"

Application

Take a look at your current pace. Are you feeling rushed, restless, or burnt out? What have you said "yes" to that God never asked you to carry?

Choose one thing to pause or release this week. Create intentional space for rest, not as a reward for productivity, but as a response to God's presence.

Prayer

Jesus, teach me to walk with you, not ahead, not behind, but in step with your Spirit. Help me resist the pull of hurry and trust the pace of grace. Let my life reflect your peace, not my pressure. I don't want to just be busy; I want to be aligned. Amen.

Guide Your Thinking:

1. *Where am I moving too fast for my soul to keep up?*

2. *What would it look like to embrace God's pace in this season?*

_____

_____

_____

_____

_____

_____

_____

_____

DAY 46
Healing from Spiritual Disappointment

Scripture

"The Lord is close to the brokenhearted and saves those who are crushed in spirit."

Psalm 34:18 (NIV)

Reflection

Spiritual disappointment is one of the quietest and most painful wounds a person can carry. It settles into the heart when prayers seem unanswered, when promises feel delayed beyond understanding, or when God appears silent in the very place you needed Him most. Perhaps you believed for healing and it did not come, or you trusted God with a dream only to watch it crumble. Maybe you were faithful, obedient, and consistent, yet life still unraveled in ways you never anticipated.

Disappointment like this does not always cause someone to walk away from faith, but it can cause something within to quietly shut down. You still show up, still say the right things, still participate in the rhythms of belief, yet beneath the surface there is a guarded place that no longer expects too much. Underneath the routine and resilience lives an unspoken question that feels almost too heavy to voice aloud: God, why did You not come through the way I believed You would?

You are not alone in asking that question. David cried out, "How long, O Lord?" in seasons of confusion and delay, and Martha said to Jesus, "If You had been here, my brother would not have died," expressing the honest grief of unmet expectation. Scripture preserves these moments to remind us that God is not threatened by our disappointment. He meets us within it, even when His purposes unfold in ways we do not yet understand.

Even Jesus wept when Lazarus died, knowing He would raise him moments later.

Grief and disappointment are not faithless; they are human. And God welcomes the full weight of your emotions. He doesn't rebuke the brokenhearted; He draws near to them.

Healing doesn't come from pretending you're okay. It comes from bringing your pain into the presence of God, not away from it. It comes from wrestling in prayer, asking hard questions, and learning to trust even when the answers don't come.

Sometimes, God's silence is not absence. Sometimes, His delays are not denials. And sometimes, the very place that hurts the most becomes the place of deepest intimacy, if you let Him meet you there.

Healing is not always instant. It's layered. It's raw. But God is patient. And He is faithful. He doesn't need you to explain your pain. He wants to sit with you in it and gently restore what's been lost.

Let Him begin that healing today.

Application

Write down an area of disappointment you've been carrying, something that still stings when you think about it. Be honest with God. You don't need polished words, just real ones.

Then, invite Him into that space. Say aloud: "God, I don't understand this... but I want to heal." Sit in stillness. Let His presence be enough for now.

Prayer

God, I've carried disappointment quietly. I've questioned Your timing and doubted Your goodness. But today, I invite You into my pain. I won't hide it anymore. Heal what I don't have words for. Show me how to trust You again, not just with my future, but with the places in my past where I felt let down. Amen.

Guide Your Thinking:

1. *Where have I been silently disappointed with God?*

2. *What would it look like to bring disappointment honestly into His presence?*

_____

_____

_____

_____

_____

_____

_____

_____

DAY 47
Carrying Peace into Chaotic Places

Scripture

"Blessed are the peacemakers, for they will be called children of God."

Matthew 5:9 (NIV)

Reflection

Peace isn't just something you feel, it's something you carry. As a follower of Jesus, you're not just called to find peace, you're called to bring it into every environment, every conversation, every atmosphere you walk into.

But let's be honest: chaos surrounds us in our homes, workplaces, churches, cities, and even in our minds. People are anxious, divided, and overwhelmed. And in a world where everyone seems to be reacting, posting, shouting, and defending, God is looking for people who are rooted, steady, and still. People who embody His peace so deeply, it shifts the room.

Jesus didn't promise peace in the absence of trouble. He promised peace in the middle of it. In John 14:27, He said, "My peace I give you. I do not give to you as the world gives." The world offers escape. Jesus offers endurance. The world offers noise. He offers stillness.

To carry peace is not to deny reality, it's to live from a deeper one. It's knowing that the Kingdom is unshaken even when the culture is shaken. It's choosing gentleness over sarcasm. Listening instead of reacting. Praying instead of panicking.

And this peace isn't passive. It's active. Peacemakers aren't avoiders, they're build-ers. They step into hard conversations, not to dominate but to disarm. They bring clarity in confusion, calm in conflict, and love where there's been division.

To carry peace is to carry the presence of Jesus. That doesn't mean you'll always feel peaceful. But it means you're anchored. You know who holds your heart. You're not tossed by every crisis. You've learned to exhale anxiety and inhale truth.

So the question isn't, "Is there chaos around me?" The question is, "What kind of spirit am I bringing into it?"

You have access to a peace the world can't give, and you have the power to bring that peace into places that desperately need it.

Application

Identify one space in your life that feels especially chaotic, your home, your schedule, a relationship, or even your own thoughts.

Ask: "What would it look like for me to carry peace here instead of anxiety?"

Then do one practical thing to shift the atmosphere, pause before speaking, pray before reacting, offer kindness where there's tension.

Prayer

Jesus, You are the Prince of Peace. I invite Your peace to rule in me so that it can flow through me. Help me carry Your calm presence into every space I enter. Make me a peacemaker, bold in love, grounded in truth, and steady in You. Amen.

Guide Your Thinking:

1. *Where in my life am I being called to bring peace instead of waiting to feel it?*

2. *How can I cultivate a deeper internal stillness that overflows into others?*

_____

_____

_____

_____

_____

_____

_____

_____

DAY 48
Building Emotional Maturity in Christ

Scripture

"Like a city whose walls are broken through is a person who lacks self-control."

Proverbs 25:28 (NIV)

Reflection

Emotional maturity is one of the clearest signs of spiritual maturity. It's not about suppressing emotions or pretending everything's fine. It's about being rooted enough in Christ that your emotions serve you, rather than control you.

We often measure growth by what we know or what we do. But God is equally interested in how we respond to pressure, disappointment, offense, and success. Because your emotional life isn't separate from your spiritual life, it's deeply connected.

The fruit of the Spirit, love, joy, peace, patience, kindness, goodness, faithfulness, gentleness, and self-control, isn't just for moments of quiet devotion. It's for the moments that trigger you, test you, or tempt you to react in ways that don't reflect who you are in Christ.

Proverbs compare a person without self-control to a city with broken walls, vulnerable, exposed, and easily overtaken. That's what happens when our emotional life goes unchecked. We become reactive instead of responsive.

Defensive instead of discerning. We let temporary emotions make permanent decisions.

Jesus was the most emotionally mature person who ever lived. He wept. He got angry. He rejoiced. But His emotions were always aligned with the Father's will. He never lashed out impulsively or let pain distort His purpose. And as His followers, we're invited to grow in that same emotional strength, not by our own effort, but through abiding in Him.

Emotional maturity means noticing your reactions and inviting the Holy Spirit into them. It means asking, "What's really going on underneath this emotion? What lie might I be believing? What truth do I need to anchor myself in?"

It's not about perfection. It's about progress. Each time you pause, pray, and choose truth over impulse, you're building walls of strength around your life, walls of wisdom, peace, and Spirit-led self-control.

The more emotionally mature you become, the more safe, steady, and powerful your presence becomes in a world that desperately needs stability.

Application

Think of a recent moment when your emotions got the best of you. What triggered it? What was the root beneath the reaction?

Ask the Holy Spirit to show you one area where He wants to grow your emotional maturity. Then, invite Him to renew your mind and give you greater awareness and self-control in that area.

Prayer

Holy Spirit, I surrender my emotional life to You. Teach me to recognize what I feel but not be ruled by it. Grow in me the fruit of self-control, wisdom, and gentleness. Make me steady, anchored, and emotionally mature, not just for my sake, but for the sake of those around me. Amen.

Guide Your Thinking:

1. *What emotions tend to lend me more than they should?*

2. *How can I practice slowing down and inviting God into my emotional reactions?*

_____

_____

_____

_____

_____

_____

_____

_____

DAY 49
Living Authentically
Before God and Others

Scripture

"Surely you desire truth in the inner parts; you teach me wisdom in the inmost place."

Psalm 51:6 (NIV)

Reflection

Authenticity is more than honesty; it's alignment. It's living in such a way that who you are privately, publicly, emotionally, and spiritually matches. It's refusing to wear masks before God or people. And it's one of the most freeing, powerful ways to reflect Christ.

God is not impressed by performance; He is drawn to truth. Psalm 51:6 says, "Surely you desire truth in the inner parts." That means He isn't just after polished prayers or perfect behavior. He desires the real you, the questions, the mess, the struggle, and the longing underneath it all.

Living authentically starts with how you come to God. Are you pretending, or are you present? Are you performing, or are you honest? True intimacy with God begins when you stop trying to impress Him and start inviting Him into every part of your story, even the parts you've tried to hide.

Authenticity doesn't mean broadcasting every thought or flaw. It means your public life matches your private one. It's having a heart posture that says, "I don't want to appear godly, I want to be godly. I want to be whole, not just well-liked."

Jesus never asked His followers to be impressive. He asked them to be real. The Pharisees knew how to put on a spiritual show, but Jesus saw right through it. He honored those who came to Him humbly: the tax collector, the woman at the well, and the bleeding woman. Their brokenness didn't repel Him. It moved Him.

There's something powerful about being truly seen and still deeply loved. And when you live that way, unmasked and surrendered, you give others permission to do the same. Your authenticity creates space for healing, honesty, and transformation in the people around you.

So take the risk of being real. Not just with God, but with trusted friends, mentors, and your community. Let them see your progress and your process. Let your life tell the truth, not just about where you've been, but about who God is making you to be.

Because the world doesn't need more polished Christians. It needs people whose lives reflect the raw, redemptive power of the gospel.

Application

Reflect on areas of your life where you feel the pressure to pretend, whether spiritually, relationally, or emotionally.

Ask God: "Where am I wearing a mask?" Then take one step today to be more honest, with God, with yourself, or with someone safe.

Prayer

God, I want to live fully known and fully loved. Help me let go of the pressure to impress and instead embrace the freedom to be real. Strip away the masks I've worn and meet me in my honesty. Teach me to walk in truth, in my heart and in my relationships. Amen.

Guide Your Thinking:

1. *Where in my life am I tempted to hide or perform instead of be real?*

2. *What does living authentically before God actually look like in my day-to-day life?*

_____

_____

_____

_____

_____

_____

_____

_____

END OF WEEK 7
Rooted in Real Transformation

You've just completed seven weeks of intentional growth. That's forty-nine days of soul work, stretching, listening, reflecting, and responding. This wasn't a journey of surface change; it was one of substance. And this week, you've been invited to live more deeply aligned with Christ, in your pace, your emotions, your story, your posture, and your presence.

You've learned that consistency in character matters more than momentary success. That healing often begins with honesty. That true peace isn't just something to receive, it's something to carry. That your emotional life is deeply tied to your spiritual life. And that authenticity isn't weakness, it's strength wrapped in surrender.

God is not forming you to impress others. He's forming you to become whole. To live with integrity. To walk in wisdom. To reflect His heart when no one else is watching. That's real transformation, and it rarely happens overnight. But step by step, word by word, decision by decision, you're being made new.

If this week brought moments of conviction, don't run from them. Lean in. If it stirred hope, nurture it. If it exposed inconsistencies, thank God, because awareness is the first step to a breakthrough.

You are not who you were on Day 1. You are becoming, more rooted, more aware, more Spirit-led. And the fruit of that will reach far beyond you.

As you prepare to enter the final stretch, don't rush. Let this week settle in your spirit. Ask God to seal the truths that resonated. And commit to finishing this journey with the same courage and surrender that brought you here.

Key Questions to Guide Your Thinking:

1. *What part of my life has become more aligned with the heart of Christ this week?*

2. *Where am I still resisting transformation, and what might be holding me back?*

3. *How can I carry these lessons into my everyday decisions in the final stretch?*

_____

_____

_____

_____

_____

_____

_____

_____

_____

_____

_____

_____

_____

Journal

WEEK 8

DAY 50
Living with Intentionality

Scripture

"Be very careful, then, how you live, not as unwise but as wise, making the most of every opportunity..."

Ephesians 5:15–16 (NIV)

Reflection

Intentionality is about living on purpose, not by pressure, not by default, and not on autopilot. It's about choosing your direction instead of drifting. And in the Kingdom of God, intentional living is an act of worship.

Paul's words in Ephesians are a wake-up call: "Be very careful how you live..." In other words, don't sleepwalk through life. Don't waste the days you've been given. Don't let culture, comparison, or comfort set your pace. Make the most of every opportunity, not just big ones, but the daily, hidden ones that shape who you're becoming.

Intentionality asks:

1. *What am I building with my time?*

2. *What voices am I allowing to shape me?*

3. *Am I living in alignment with what I truly value, or just reacting to what's urgent?*

Jesus lived with radical intentionality. Every moment had weight. Every word was purposeful. He didn't rush, but He didn't waste time either. He knew when to say yes, when to rest, when to walk away, and when to press in. His life was full, but never frantic.

Living with intentionality doesn't mean you have every step planned. It means you're anchored. It means you wake up with vision and live with discernment. It means you stop chasing everyone else's "should" and start living from the calling God has placed in your life.

It's easy to get swept up in survival mode, going through the motions, checking off tasks, numbing with distraction. But intentionality says, "My days are a gift. My choices matter. My life is a seed that will bear fruit, one way or another."

This doesn't mean adding pressure. It means gaining clarity. You don't have to do everything, but you're called to do something with purpose. And the more intentional you become, the more peace and joy you'll carry. Because you're no longer chasing, you're building.

Application

Take time to examine your current routines, relationships, and responsibilities. Ask: "Are these aligned with the life God is calling me to build?"

Choose one area (time, relationships, faith practices, boundaries) where you can live more intentionally this week. Make a small, measurable shift that brings alignment.

Prayer

Father, teach me to number my days and live with wisdom. I don't want to drift; I want to build. Help me live on purpose, fully awake to what You're doing in and through me. Show me where I've become reactive instead of intentional, and lead me into rhythms that reflect Your Kingdom. Amen.

Guide Your Thinking:

1. *Where in my life am I drifting instead of living with direction?*

2. *What's one decision I can make today to live with greater intention?*

_____

_____

_____

_____

_____

_____

_____

_____

DAY 51
Walking with Wisdom in Daily Decisions

Scripture

"If any of you lacks wisdom, you should ask God, who gives generously to all without finding fault, and it will be given to you."

James 1:5 (NIV)

Reflection

Life is made of decisions, some loud and life-changing, others quiet and habitual. But together, they shape your direction. And while the world offers countless voices telling you what to do, wisdom teaches you to first ask: "God, what is best, not just what is easy or expected?"

James tells us that God gives wisdom generously. He's not withholding it. He's not playing games. But often, we don't ask, not because we don't care, but because we're moving too fast or trusting our own instincts more than His insight.

Wisdom isn't just about intellect or experience; it's about alignment. It's knowing how to apply truth in real time. It's the Spirit-led ability to discern timing, motives, impact, and eternal value in everyday choices. From how you handle conflict, to how you spend money, to what you say yes or no to, wisdom matters.

Proverbs remind us that wisdom cries out in the streets (Proverbs 1:20). In other words, God's guidance is not locked away for the spiritually elite. It's available to anyone who will pause long enough to listen.

Jesus lived with perfect wisdom. He navigated crowds, responded to critics, chose His moments with intention, and never let pressure override discernment. He didn't rush. He didn't over-explain. He walked in step with heaven's wisdom at every turn.

And as His follower, you have access to that same Spirit of wisdom. The Holy Spirit longs to guide you, not just in crisis, but in the daily rhythm of life. He's present when you choose how to spend your time, who you give your attention to, what you commit to, and how you respond under pressure.

But wisdom requires humility. It means admitting you don't know everything, and that's okay. It means slowing down to ask God before assuming or acting. It means trading impulse for insight, emotion for discernment, and pressure for prayer.

Today, let wisdom lead. It may not be the loudest voice, but it will always be the truest one.

Application

Think about one decision, big or small, you're facing right now. Instead of analyzing it endlessly, pause and ask God directly: "What is wise?"

Open scripture. Listen. Journal. Don't just ask once; create a habit of seeking wisdom daily. Write down any promptings, confirmations, or scriptures that rise up.

Prayer

God, I need Your wisdom today, not just for the big decisions, but for the little ones that shape my path. Teach me to pause, to ask, to listen, and to trust Your guidance. Let wisdom be my compass, not my emotions or expectations. Help me walk in step with Your Spirit. Amen.

Guide Your Thinking:

1. *Where in my life am I making decisions without first seeking God's wisdom?*

2. *What would change if I slowed down and asked, "What's wise?" more often?*

_____

_____

_____

_____

_____

_____

_____

_____

_____

DAY 52
Embracing God's Timing When Life Feels Slow

Scripture

"There is a time for everything, and a season for every activity under the heavens."

Ecclesiastes 3:1 (NIV)

Reflection

Waiting is rarely easy, especially in a culture that celebrates speed, productivity, and visible results. We are conditioned to equate movement with progress and immediacy with success, so when outcomes are delayed and timelines stretch beyond our expectations, frustration often follows. We want clarity, confirmation, and closure, yet God does not operate according to our hurried pace. His timing is flawless and intentional, but from our limited perspective it can feel uncomfortably slow and even disorienting.

It is within these in between seasons, when circumstances appear unchanged and prayers seem unanswered, that our trust is truly examined and our faith is carefully shaped. Waiting exposes what we genuinely believe about God's character, His sovereignty, and His goodness. In these quiet stretches of uncertainty, spiritual maturity either deepens as we lean into Him or drifts as we allow impatience to take root. The delay is not wasted time but sacred ground where endurance is developed, motives are refined, and dependence on God grows stronger.

Scripture consistently reminds us that waiting has always been part of God's redemptive story. Abraham waited decades for the promised son who would fulfill God's covenant. Joseph endured betrayal, false accusation, and imprisonment before stepping into the position God had prepared for him. David was anointed king long before he ever wore the crown, spending years in obscurity and adversity before the promise manifested. Their stories reveal that waiting is not a detour from purpose but often the very process through which purpose is prepared and sustained.

Jesus waited in silence for thirty years before public ministry.

These weren't wasted seasons; they were preparation seasons. Seasons where character was forged, intimacy with God was deepened, and dependence was strengthened. What may feel slow to you is often strategic to Him.

God is never late. But He's also rarely early. His timing works on a different level, woven with wisdom, purpose, and eternal vision. While you wait, He's not just preparing the outcome; He's preparing you. He's aligning relationships, stretching your character, healing things you didn't know needed healing.

The slowness you feel might actually be the safety of His pace.

When life feels delayed, you have two choices: become bitter in the pause or become better in the process. One leads to anxiety, striving, and control. The other leads to surrender, peace, and renewed strength.

Waiting doesn't mean doing nothing. It means doing the next right thing, faithfully, prayerfully, with open hands. It means believing God is still working, even in what you cannot see.

Today, instead of asking, "When will this change?", ask, "What are you teaching me while I wait?"

Application

Reflect on an area of your life that feels slow or stalled. Write down what emotions the delay is stirring in you: frustration, fear, fatigue?

Ask God: "What do You want to grow in me during this season?"

Then, choose one act of faithfulness you can do today while you wait, however small.

Prayer

Father, I don't always understand Your timing, but I choose to trust it. Help me surrender the rush, the pressure, and the fear of delay. Teach me to see the slowness as sacred. Grow in me a heart that waits well, with peace, expectancy, and faith. Amen.

Guide Your Thinking:

1. *What delay in my life is challenging my trust in God's timing?*

2. *How can I lean into this season as preparation, not punishment?*

_____

_____

_____

_____

_____

_____

_____

_____

_____

DAY 53
The Gift of Spiritual Friendships

Scripture

"As iron sharpens iron, so one person sharpens another."

Proverbs 27:17 (NIV)

Reflection

God never designed you to walk this journey alone. From the very beginning, we were created for connection, not shallow, surface-level relationships, but deep, soul-sharpening friendships that point us back to truth and forward in purpose.

Spiritual friendship is a gift, sacred and rare. It's more than shared interests or life stage compatibility. It's a relationship rooted in Christ, shaped by grace, and anchored in mutual growth. These are the friends who don't just make you laugh; they help you live. They pray with you, challenge you, call out your gifts, and hold up your arms when you're tired.

Proverbs says, "As iron sharpens iron..." Sharpening implies friction. It means sometimes your spiritual friends won't tell you what you want to hear, but what you need to hear. And yet, it's spoken in love. In safety. In covenant.

Jesus had spiritual friends. He didn't isolate. He lived closely with people who knew His rhythms, His struggles, and His mission. He shared meals, tears, and prayers with them. And in His most vulnerable moments, He didn't ask for a sermon, He asked them to stay with Him.

You need those kinds of people. And you need to be that kind of person.

Spiritual friendships require vulnerability. Intentionality. Forgiveness. They're not always easy. But when centered on Christ, they become one of the greatest sources of strength, joy, and accountability in your walk with God.

If you've been walking alone, pray for this kind of friendship. If you have it, nurture it. And if you've been wounded in relationships, let God heal you so you can trust again.

Faith was never meant to be lived in isolation. Some of your deepest breakthroughs may come through the voice of a trusted friend who sees what you forgot about yourself and reminds you of who you really are.

Application

Take time today to reflect on your current friendships. Who in your life encourages you spiritually? Who holds you accountable in love?

Reach out to one spiritual friend this week, thank them, encourage them, or pray with them. And if you're lacking this kind of connection, ask God to open doors and give you the courage to pursue it.

Prayer

God, thank You for the gift of relationships rooted in You. Teach me how to cultivate and honor spiritual friendships. Give me the humility to be sharpened and the courage to sharpen others. Help me build connections that reflect Your love, challenge me toward growth, and draw us all closer to You. Amen.

Guide Your Thinking:

1. *Who in my life challenges me spiritually and reminds me of God's truth?*

2. *How can I be a better spiritual friend to someone else?*

_____

_____

_____

_____

_____

_____

_____

_____

DAY 54
Becoming Resilient Through Spiritual Perseverance

Scripture

"Let perseverance finish its work so that you may be mature and complete, not lacking anything."

James 1:4 (NIV)

Reflection

There are seasons when faith feels like fire, burning bright, passionate, and alive. But there are also seasons when faith feels more like a flicker, carried by nothing but perseverance, the choice to keep going when everything in you wants to quit.

Spiritual perseverance is not flashy. It's not always loud or emotional. It's the quiet, daily decision to stay faithful. To keep showing up in prayer when answers haven't come. To keep loving when it isn't reciprocated. To keep believing when a breakthrough feels distant.

James tells us that perseverance does something profound: it finishes the work of transformation. It shapes maturity. It builds a kind of faith that isn't based on feeling, but on a foundation. It's not just about making it through pain; it's about becoming someone new in the process.

We don't talk about perseverance enough. But it's one of the clearest marks of spiritual growth. Anyone can worship when life is good. But it takes resilient faith to keep worshipping in the wilderness. It takes spiritual stamina to love when you're tired, to serve when you feel unseen, to hope when you feel dry.

Perseverance doesn't deny difficulty; it walks through it with purpose. It says, "This is hard. But God is still worthy." It transforms suffering into strength, not by removing the trial, but by refining you in it.

Jesus endured the cross because of the joy set before Him. Paul endured prison with songs on his mouth. Ruth persevered through loss and became part of Christ's lineage. The story of scripture is filled with people who didn't give up, even when they had every reason to.

And you are part of that same story.

Resilience doesn't mean you don't cry. It means you don't quit. It means you trust that God is still working, even in the waiting and the weariness. Your faith doesn't have to be loud to be strong. Sometimes, it just has to last.

Application

Think of one area in your life right now where you're tempted to give up, check out, or pull back.

Ask God: "What are You forming in me through this?"

Then, choose one practical way to persevere today, even if it's small. One prayer. One step. One act of faithfulness.

Prayer

Lord, I'm tired, but I want to be faithful. Help me endure not with bitterness, but with hope. Build in me a resilient spirit. Strengthen my resolve. Let perseverance finish its work in me, so that I may be complete, fully Yours, no matter the season. Amen.

Guide Your Thinking:

1. *Where in my life do I need fresh strength to keep going?*

2. *What would it look like to persevere with joy, not just endurance?*

_____

_____

_____

_____

_____

_____

_____

_____

_____

DAY 55
Rebuilding Trust After It's Been Broken

Scripture

"Above all, love each other deeply, because love covers over a multitude of sins."

1 Peter 4:8 (NIV)

Reflection

Trust is fragile. It takes years to build, and only a moment to shatter. Whether it's the bonds we form with others, our own self-assurance, or even our walk with God, broken trust leaves behind a fracture that can feel impossible to mend. Maybe someone let you down. Maybe you let yourself down. Maybe you trusted God and the outcome wasn't what you hoped. In every case, the pain of that rupture can breed walls of fear and whisper that it's safer never to open your heart again.

But we serve a God who specializes in restoration, including trust. Healing begins with honesty: naming the hurt, bringing it before Him, and refusing to numb or bury it. The wound is real, but so is the promise of new life. Sometimes restoration looks like reconciliation with another person. Sometimes it's learning to forgive yourself. And sometimes it's about allowing God to reshape your view of Him, not through the lens of past disappointments, but through the lens of His unchanging truth.

Rebuilding trust is slow work. It demands grace, clear communication, healthy boundaries, and patience. Above all, it demands hope, faith that healing is possible and that God can breathe beauty into every fracture. If a relationship can't be restored to its former shape, your heart can still heal. If your trust in God has been shaken, He is not intimidated by your questions or hesitations; He sits with you in the rubble, gently and faithfully recreating safety from the ruins.

Let's say the quiet part out loud: trust is earned on both sides. Some people don't deserve it again, and if we're honest, neither do we. We've all failed to lie, to walk away, to be absent when someone needed us most. Someone has done the same to us, too, leaving behind questions without answers and pain without apologies. Scripture calls us to rebuild, but it isn't a matter of flipping a spiritual switch or reciting the right verse. True trust rebirths only when something dies: our pride, their denial, our illusion of control, and sometimes even our hope of full understanding.

Forgiveness is free, but trust is expensive. When Peter wept, Jesus forgave him instantly, but that trust was slowly restored by the rhythm of faithful presence: showing up, feeding sheep, staying the course. If you've broken trust, stop demanding belief and start becoming trustworthy. Show consistency over time, embrace accountability without manipulation, and repent even when nobody applauds your progress. And if you've been betrayed, remember that forgiveness and healthy boundaries can coexist. Saying, "I forgive you, but I need space before I can trust again," is not bitterness; it's wise stewardship of your heart.

Rebuilding trust is sacred work, unremarkable, unglamorous, and never instant. But when undertaken with humility, truth, and hope, it becomes a resurrection story waiting to be told. There is life after broken trust. There is love. There is hope. And it all begins when we surrender our fractures into the hands of the One who makes all things new.

Application

Start today by looking inward and asking yourself in the same breath, "Where am I asking for trust I haven't earned, and where am I withholding trust not out of discernment but out of fear or revenge?" As you sit with those questions, choose one concrete step, no matter how small, that moves you toward healing rather than toward the safety of old comforts. Recall a place where trust was broken in your life, whether in a friendship, in your own self-confidence, or in your walk with God, and give yourself permission to write freely about what that fracture cost you and what you've been afraid to hope for again.

When your words have laid bare both the pain and the possibilities, turn your heart heavenward and pray: "God, I invite You into this broken place. Show me how to heal, how to forgive, and how to trust again, wisely, slowly, and in step with Your truth." Let this single, honest exercise become your roadmap out of the rubble and into the hope of restoration.

Ask this brutally honest question: "Where am I asking for trust I haven't earned?"

Then ask the mirror version: "Where am I withholding trust not out of discernment, but out of fear or revenge?"

Choose one step today that reflects movement toward healing, not toward comfort.

Someone you've seen before used to talk about change but never follow through. They lied to cover shame, then apologized to avoid the consequences. But lately? They've stopped explaining and started doing. Quietly. Repeatedly. That's what rebuilding looks like.

Prayer

God, I've failed people. And I've been failed. Teach me how to love wisely, truthfully, courageously, and patiently. Help me own my part when I've broken trust. And help me forgive without losing my soul. Rebuild what's been shattered, one costly step at a time. Amen.

Guide Your Thinking:

1. *Where has trust been broken, and what would healing actually require?*

2. *What does it look like to rebuild trust without pretending nothing happened?*

_____

_____

_____

_____

_____

_____

_____

_____

DAY 56
Letting Go of the Fear of Man

Scripture

"Fear of man will prove to be a snare, but whoever trusts in the Lord is kept safe."

Proverbs 29:25 (NIV)

Reflection

Few things shape our decisions more subtly or more powerfully than the fear of what others think. It doesn't always show up as obvious anxiety. Sometimes, it sounds like second-guessing yourself after you speak. Avoiding hard conversations. Shrinking back from what God asked you to do. Saying "yes" when you meant "no."

This fear can mask itself as politeness, diplomacy, or humility. But underneath, it's often insecurity, rooted in the belief that our worth rises and falls based on people's opinions.

Proverbs is clear: the fear of man is a snare. A trap. It will keep you small. Keep you quiet. Keep you performing. You'll begin shaping your life to avoid rejection rather than to fulfill purpose.

And here's the thing: no matter how hard you try, you will never please everyone. Someone will always misunderstand, critique, or question you. Even Jesus, the perfect, sinless Son of God, was rejected, doubted, and betrayed.

But Jesus didn't waver. Why? Because He knew who He was and whose He was. He didn't live for crowds, He lived from His Father's voice. That's how He could speak truth in love, walk away from false expectations, and stay steady in the face of rejection.

When you're secure in God's love, you're no longer held hostage by human approval. You stop editing yourself to fit in. You stop living for likes, compliments, or validation. You live from a deeper place, a place of identity and authority.

This doesn't mean becoming harsh or closed off. It means becoming free. Free to disappoint people if it means obeying God. Free to lead without applause. Free to rest when others want more. Free to be misunderstood without unraveling.

Letting go of the fear of man isn't about becoming fearless, it's about choosing faith instead. Trusting that God's approval outweighs the criticism, silence, or misunderstanding of others. Trusting that when you stand in His will, you stand in strength.

If your heart has been entangled in the need to please, God isn't condemning you. He's inviting you out. Into clarity. Into courage. Into the quiet, unshakable joy of living for an audience of One.

Application

Ask the Holy Spirit to reveal areas where you've been living for approval, big or small. Write down one place where fear of people's opinions has silenced, slowed, or shaped you.

Pray through it, then speak this declaration aloud: "I am no longer a slave to the fear of man. I live for the voice of God, and His approval is enough for me."

Repeat as needed, until truth sinks deeper than fear.

Prayer

Lord, I've been swayed too often by what others think. But today, I want to be anchored in what You say. Set me free from the snare of people-pleasing. Teach me to walk in courage, humility, and spiritual authority. Let Your voice be the loudest one in my life. I live for You alone. Amen.

Guide Your Thinking:

1. *In what ways have I allowed fear of others to shape how I speak, serve, or show up?*

2. *What would it feel like to live free, rooted in God's love, not in people's praise?*

DAY 57
Anchored by Conviction in a Compromised Culture

Scripture

"Do not conform to the pattern of this world, but be transformed by the renewing of your mind..."

Romans 12:2 (NIV)

Reflection

Conviction is more than a strong opinion; it's a spiritual anchor. It's the deep, inner resolve to live aligned with God's truth, even when it costs you something, especially when it costs you something.

In today's world, truth is treated like clay, molded by preference, bent by emotion, and shaped by culture. We're constantly told to follow our hearts, embrace our truth, and avoid offending anyone. But the Kingdom of God isn't built on personal truth; it's built on eternal truth. And eternal truth doesn't bend to culture, it transforms it.

Paul's words in Romans 12:2 are urgent: "Do not conform to the pattern of this world." Why? Because the world has a pattern, a current, and if you're not intentional, you'll be swept into it without even noticing. Compromise rarely begins with outright rebellion. It starts with a softening of your stance. A silent yes to things you once resisted. A slow drift from conviction to convenience.

But conviction pulls you back to the center. It reminds you of who you are, whose you are, and what you're called to carry. It gives you the courage to say "no" when it's unpopular and "yes" when it's risky. And it doesn't just protect your integrity, it reflects your God.

Look at Daniel, taken from his home, immersed in a pagan culture, offered comfort, power, and status. But he resolved not to defile himself. He didn't cause a scene. He simply stood firm. And God honored it. He gave Daniel influence not in spite of his conviction, but because of it.

The same is true for you. God isn't looking for perfect people; He's looking for faithful ones. People who live with quiet courage. Who doesn't trade purity for popularity? Who chooses holiness over hype? Who live like eternity matters more than applause.

Conviction isn't about judgment or superiority. It's about alignment. It's the result of being so deeply formed by God's Word that you're no longer swayed by every opinion, trend, or temptation.

And here's the beauty: when you live anchored by conviction, people notice. Not because you're loud, but because you're different. Grounded. Unshakeable. There's a power in that kind of life, and it starts by renewing your mind and realigning your heart every single day.

Application

Ask God to search your heart today. Where have you slowly compromised? Where are your values being shaped more by culture than by Christ?

Write down one conviction you want to re-anchor. Then make one small, courageous decision that reflects that truth this week, whether it's in a conversation, a boundary, or a quiet act of obedience.

Prayer

Lord, I don't want to drift; I want to be anchored. Forgive me for the places where I've softened my stance to avoid discomfort or fit in. Renew my mind. Align my heart with Your truth. Give me the courage to live with quiet conviction and bold love, no matter the cost. Amen.

Guide Your Thinking:

1. *What have I begun to compromise, through silence, apathy, or fear?*

2. *What would it look like for me to live with conviction and compassion this week?*

_____

_____

_____

_____

_____

_____

_____

_____

DAY 58
Practicing Sacred Joy in the Midst of Ordinary Life

Scripture

"The joy of the Lord is your strength."

Nehemiah 8:10 (NIV)

Reflection

Joy often gets mistaken for something loud and momentary, a celebration, a high, a breakthrough. But in the Kingdom of God, joy is much deeper. It's not reserved for mountaintop moments or rare victories. Joy is sacred. And it's meant to be practiced, especially in the middle of ordinary, unremarkable days.

Nehemiah spoke those words, "The joy of the Lord is your strength", to people who had just come face-to-face with their failures. They had repented. They were tired. But instead of calling for sorrow, Nehemiah called for joy. Why? Because joy doesn't come from perfection, it comes from the presence of God.

Sacred joy is different than fleeting happiness. It's not dependent on external circumstances. It's born from deep trust, knowing God is with you, working through you, and sustaining you, even when life feels mundane or heavy.

The truth is most of life is lived in the ordinary. Laundry piles. Emails. Errands. Conversations. Dishes. And it's easy to believe that joy only lives in the big moments. But sacred joy meets you in the kitchen, in the quiet, in the repetition. It transforms your normal into holy ground, not because of what's happening, but because of who is with you in it.

Practicing joy means learning to notice. To slow down. To celebrate small wins. To savor a moment of silence. To choose gratitude over grumbling. It's not denial of pain; it's defiance against despair. It's looking your chaos in the eye and choosing to smile anyway, not because everything is good, but because God is still good.

Jesus carried joy. Hebrews tells us that "for the joy set before Him, He endured the cross." That joy wasn't circumstantial; it was deeply rooted in purpose, in love, and in the eternal hope of what was to come. You're invited into that same kind of joy. Not a performance, but a presence. Not hype, but holy strength.

So today, don't wait for life to get easier or more exciting to embrace joy. Practice it. Cultivate it. Choose it, right where you are.

Application

Take inventory of your current emotional rhythm. Have you been ignoring joy because life feels too busy, stressful, or unremarkable?

Write down five small things that bring you joy. Ask God to meet you in those spaces. Then take one small, joyful action today, something simple but intentional. Let it be an act of worship.

Prayer

God, I don't want to live numb or distracted. Teach me to practice joy, not as a reaction, but as a rhythm. Let Your presence awaken delight in the middle of my ordinary life. Fill me with joy that doesn't fade with circumstances but grows with every step of trust. Amen.

Guide Your Thinking:

1. *What does sacred joy look like in my current season?*

2. *How can I practice joy intentionally, even in the middle of what feels repetitive or hard?*

_____

_____

_____

_____

_____

_____

_____

_____

_____

DAY 59
Cultivating a Legacy of Quiet Faithfulness

Scripture

"His master replied, 'Well done, good and faithful servant! You have been faithful with a few things..."

Matthew 25:21 (NIV)

Reflection

In a world that prizes visibility, platform, and instant impact, quiet faithfulness can feel... invisible. Unnoticed. Underappreciated. But in the Kingdom of God, quiet faithfulness is not only seen, it's celebrated.

Jesus didn't say, "Well done, successful servant," or "Well done, famous servant." He said, "Well done, good and faithful servant." Faithfulness is the metric of heaven. It's not about how impressive your life looks; it's about how consistent your "yes" is behind the scenes.

Quiet faithfulness is raising children in love when no one sees your sacrifice. It's showing up to serve when it's not glamorous.

It's praying behind closed doors, sowing seeds of kindness, forgiving when it's hard, and staying steady in the same direction when walking away would be easier.

This kind of legacy isn't built in a moment; it's built over time. Small decisions. Repeated obedience. Years of walking with God, when you feel inspired and when you don't. These are the lives that leave eternal impact, not because they were loud, but because they were rooted.

Noah spent decades building an ark before a single drop of rain fell. Ruth stayed loyal through loss. Anna prayed in the temple for decades before seeing the Messiah. Their stories weren't spectacular in the world's eyes, but they were sacred in God's.

You don't need to go viral to be valuable. You don't need to be known by the world to be remembered by heaven. What you do in secret, when no one's watching, matters more than you know. It is forming a legacy, brick by brick, of a life that reflects God's faithfulness.

Don't despise your slow progress or quiet obedience. Every unseen act of love, every prayer whispered in faith, every time you choose forgiveness over bitterness, it's building something eternal.

Live for that "well done."

Application

Reflect on the rhythms of your daily life. Where have you been faithful, even when it's gone unseen?

Thank God for the strength to stay consistent. Write a note to yourself (or someone else) honoring that quiet faithfulness. Let it be a reminder that the small things do matter.

Prayer

God, help me stay faithful. Not for recognition but because you are worthy of my steady love. Remind me that what's done in secret is never wasted in Your Kingdom. Shape my legacy not through fame but through faithfulness. May I finish well, one faithful step at a time. Amen.

Guide Your Thinking:

1. *Where have I been faithful without seeing fruit yet?*

2. *How might God be using my quiet obedience to shape a legacy beyond what I can see?*

_____

_____

_____

_____

_____

_____

_____

_____

DAY 60
A Life Fully Surrendered
The Journey of Becoming

Scripture

"Therefore, I urge you, brothers and sisters, in view of God's mercy, to offer your bodies as a living sacrifice, holy and pleasing to God, this is your true and proper worship."

Romans 12:1 (NIV)

Reflection

You've come to the final day of this journey. Sixty days of showing up, seeking God, sitting in hard truths, soaking in grace, being stretched, challenged, encouraged, and loved. You've unlearned old habits, embraced deeper rhythms, and allowed your heart to be reshaped by the Spirit.

But this isn't the end. It's the beginning of a new way of living. A life not built around performance, pressure, or perfection but around presence. A life marked by surrender.

Paul's words in Romans 12 are an invitation to a new way of being: "Offer your bodies as a living sacrifice..." Not a one-time offering. Not just your Sunday self. But your whole life, your thoughts, your schedule, your habits, your relationships, your dreams. Everything.

Surrender isn't a loss; it's a trade. You're giving up control, but you're gaining peace. You're laying down fear and picking up purpose.

You're saying "no" to living for applause and "yes" to living for the One who already calls you beloved.

And this journey of becoming? It doesn't happen in a single moment. It happens through daily decisions to return to Jesus. To choose the narrow path. To keep your heart soft, your ears open, and your hands lifted.

You may not feel "finished." You may still feel messy. That's okay. Becoming is not about arrival; it's about staying in step with the One who's walking with you. Transformation is slow. But every surrendered step leads to deeper joy, greater freedom, and unshakable identity.

Today is your invitation to live fully surrendered. Not just as a devotional practice, but as a life posture. Let every part of you be an offering. Let your days reflect the beauty of a life yielded to grace. Let your story point to the goodness of the One who never stopped pursuing you.

You don't need to strive anymore. You just need to stay surrendered.

Application

Reread Romans 12:1 and reflect on what it means to live as a "living sacrifice." What is God asking you to surrender in this new season?

Write a prayer of commitment, your own personal declaration to live fully surrendered, not just for a season, but for a lifetime.

Prayer

God, I give You everything. Not just my words, but my time, my thoughts, my decisions, my heart. I want to live fully surrendered, not for my glory, but for Yours. Keep shaping me, refining me, and leading me. Let my life be a living offering of worship to You, every step, every breath, every moment. Amen.

Guide Your Thinking:

1. *What does a life of full surrender look like in my daily reality?*

2. *How will I carry what God has done in these 60 days into the months and years to come?*

_____

_____

_____

_____

_____

_____

_____

_____

FINAL THOUGHTS
The Becoming Never Ends

You've completed sixty days of deep reflection, truth, transformation, and pursuit. That is no small thing. But if there's one truth that echoes at the end of this journey, it's this: the becoming never ends.

These past sixty days weren't about achieving spiritual perfection; they were about awakening something eternal within you. A hunger for more of God. A tenderness to His presence. A willingness to wrestle with truth. And a desire to live fully surrendered, not just in theory, but in the small, ordinary moments of your real life.

You've learned to choose stillness in a noisy world. To persevere in silence. To live from identity, not insecurity. You've surrendered what once defined you and stepped into rhythms that anchor you. You've begun to become, more rooted, more refined, more real.

But this isn't the finish line. It's the foundation. The deeper work starts now.

Becoming is a daily rhythm. It happens in secret places, not on stages. It's forged in your yes, shaped in your surrender, refined in your repetition. Some days it looks like bold obedience. Other days, it looks like barely getting out of bed with faith still intact. But every day, it's sacred.

There will still be moments of wrestling. Seasons that feel slow. Questions that don't have quick answers. But you've now learned how to walk with God through them, not around them. You've learned that the King is not waiting at the end of your journey, He's walking beside you every step of the way.

So don't let this be the end of a devotional. Let it be the start of a life-style. A life marked by presence, by depth, by courage, by grace. A life that doesn't chase becoming for the sake of performance, but for the sake of knowing Jesus more intimately and reflecting Him more clearly.

And when you stumble, as we all do, come back. When you forget, return. When you grow weary, remember becoming is not about striving. It's about staying surrendered.

You don't need to have it all figured out. You just need to keep walking. One step at a time. One surrendered moment at a time. You are becoming.

BENEDICTION
A Blessing for Becoming

May you walk from this place not with pressure,
But with peace.
Not striving to earn,
But standing in what's already been given.

May the truth you've uncovered sink deep into your bones,
That you are known, loved, chosen, and called.
When the world tries to pull you back into the hustle,
May you remember the pace of grace.

When fear rises,
May you be anchored by the voice of your King.
When your steps feel slow,
May you know that growth is still happening
Beneath the surface.

May your heart remain tender,
Your spirit teachable,
Your convictions strong,
And your love bold.

May you continue to surrender,
Not just in the sacred moments,
But in the unseen ones,
Where true transformation is formed.

And as you go,
May the God who began a good work in you
Carry it to completion,

Day by day, Step by step,
Until you are fully, freely, And forever His.
In Jesus' name, Amen.

Let the King shape your heart, one day at a time.

The King & Me

Let the King shape your heart, one day at a time.

The King & Me is a 60-day devotional journey toward becoming more like Christ. Rooted in scripture and framed by heartfelt reflection, each daily entry is crafted to guide you deeper into God's presence and character.

Whether you're just starting your faith journey or seeking fresh spiritual rhythm, this book offers a companion through grace, growth, and truth.

www.ingramcontent.com/pod-product-compliance
Lightning Source LLC
Chambersburg PA
CBHW030919140626
46545CB00016B/1767